HIGHWAY C

Questions and A

HIGHWAY CODE Questions and Answers

Three hundred questions and answers based on the latest Highway Code, arranged to help you with your test. Over eighty "star" questions are included.

by

John Humphries, B.Sc., M.Sc.

PAPERFRONTS

Typeset in 10pt Times Roman by One & A Half Graphics, Redhill, Surrey. Printed and bound in Great Britain by Cox & Wyman Ltd., Reading, Berkshire.

The *Paperfronts* series and the *Right Way* series are both published by Elliot Right Way Books, Brighton Road, Lower Kingswood, Tadworth, Surrey, KT20 6TD, U.K.

Introduction

'Drive at a speed that will allow you to stop well within the distance you can see to be clear.'

(rule 57)

This book is for people who intend to take the driving or motorcycle tests. It contains 300 questions and answers designed to make learning the Code an easier task.

This edition is completely updated in accordance with the latest revised Code. Most of the signs and signals in this book appear in the Code. A few can be found only in its companion booklet, *Know Your Traffic Signs*, issued by the Department of Transport. All the signs can, of course, be seen on the road.

You must know the Code thoroughly to pass your test. During the test you must drive according to the rules of the Code, and the examiner will ask you several specific questions to test your knowledge of the Code.

The questions have been designed to help you to learn the Code, and are not necessarily intended to be identical to those the examiner may ask, but of course he or she may well ask similar questions.

There are more than 80 *'Star' questions* which are known to be similar to questions actually asked in the test, or which are considered to be particularly important in their own right. These questions are asterisked.

Good luck with your driving, your learning of the Code and of course your test – and never forget rule 57!

Acknowledgements

The author and publisher are grateful for the permission of the Department of Transport, and Her Majesty's Stationery Office, to reproduce a number of the drawings and road signs from the *Highway Code* and we would also like to thank them for allowing us to quote many of the rules. Wording directly reprinted has been indicated by the use of quotation marks. The author would also like to thank Theodore Rowland-Entwistle for his help in revising this latest edition.

Questions

(Answers start on page 58)

1 *Accidents:* describe any indications which may forewarn you of *an accident ahead.*

*2 *Stopping distances:* what is the overall stopping distance for a car travelling at *50 m.p.h.* on a dry road? (Answer in *metres* or feet.) Roughly how many car lengths is that?

3 *Roundabouts:* what procedure should you follow when *turning left* at a roundabout?

4 *Signals:* describe the *arm signal* you should give as a car driver to a policeman controlling traffic if you wanted to go *straight on.*

5 *Motorway lanes:* on a motorway with a *two-lane* carriageway (outside and inside lanes only), what should the two lanes be used for?

6 *Lanes:* what is the middle lane of a *three-lane single* carriageway used for?

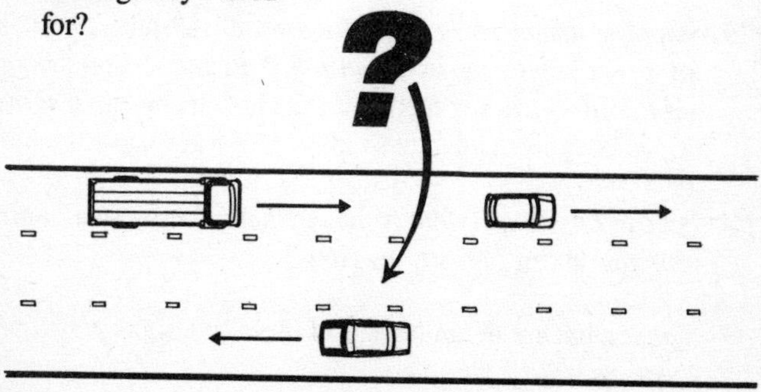

7 *Motorway prohibitions:* in what circumstances would you pick up a *hitch-hiker* on a motorway?

8 *Lights:* what must you remember about the *working and adjustments* of the lamps on your car?

9 *Signs:* what is the full meaning of this sign?

(black sign on white background)

10 *Vehicle condition:* you should always keep your vehicle in good condition; what parts *in particular* does the Highway Code stress should be kept in good condition?

***11** *Traffic lights:* give the *sequence of colours* on traffic lights.

***12** *Motorway overtaking:* are there any circumstances when it is permissible to overtake on the left?

***13** *Stopping distances:* what is the overall stopping distance for a car travelling at *30 m.p.h.*? Please express your answer in *metres* (or feet) and state how many *car lengths* this is roughly equivalent to.

***14** *Pelican crossings:* what is the difference between a *puffin crossing* and a *pelican crossing*?

15 *Signs:* what are the meanings of these five signs which all show cycles?

(a) (b)

(c) (d) (e)

((a), (b) and (e) are white cycles on blue backgrounds, (c) is a black cycle in a red circle, and (d) is a black cycle in a red triangle)

16 *Ice-cream vans:* when driving near a *parked ice-cream van*, what should you do?

17 *Kerb markings:* what is the significance of *triple yellow flashes* marked on the kerb?

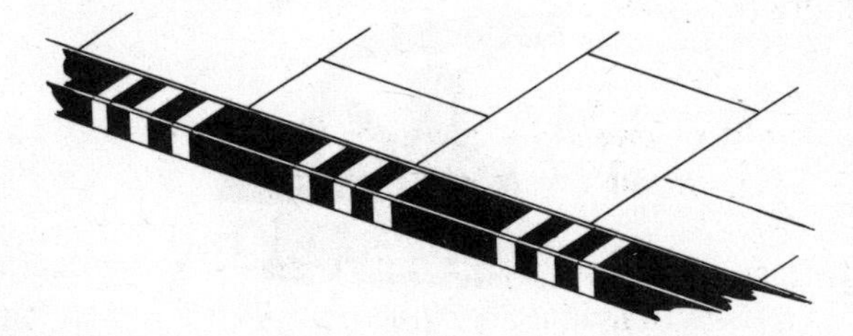

18 *Motorway procedure:* what is a *motorway*?

***19** *Lines:* what must you remember about the crossing of *double white lines* along the middle of the road if one is broken?

20 *Motorcyclists:* apart from a safety helmet, what five other things does the Highway Code say should also be worn by motorcyclists?

21 *Tiredness:* what does the Code have to say about driving and tiredness?

22 *Signs:* describe the sign meaning a *quayside* or river bank.

23 *Car telephones:* what good advice does the Code give with regard to *car telephones* and *microphones*?

24 *Signals:* what are the meanings of these three *arm signals*?

(a)

(b)

(c)

***25** *Parking:* in the Highway Code rules 138, 139, 140, 141, 142, 179 and 180 list 26 places where you must not park or stop. How many can you name?

26 *Junctions:* the Code mentions cyclists and pedestrians as being particularly at risk at junctions. What sound advice is offered?

***27** *Stopping distances:* what is the overall stopping distance for a car travelling at *20 m.p.h.*? (Answer in *metres* or *feet*.)

28 *Horn:* the Highway Code advises that you should sound your horn for *one purpose only;* what is that?

29 *Sun-glasses:* in what circumstances should you not drive wearing *sun glasses* or *similar tinted optical equipment*?

30 *Pedestrians:* it is well-known that blind people may carry white sticks. What might a *deaf/blind person carry*?

***31** *Winter driving:* what advice does the Code give about winter driving?

32 *Kerb markings:* what is the significance of *single yellow flashes* marked on the kerb?

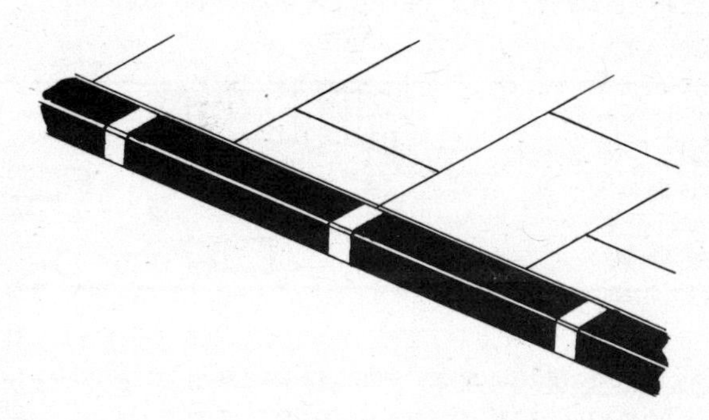

***33** *Motorway lanes:* what should the *outer lane or lanes* on a motorway be used for?

34 *Overtaking:* what advice does the Code give about overtaking *motorcyclists, pedal cyclists* and *horse riders*?

35 *Lights:* what *lights should you use* in the following circumstances:

(a) at night on lighted motorways and other roads where the speed limit exceeds 50 m.p.h.;
(b) during day-time visibility reduced by fog or snow;
(c) at dusk;
(d) in built-up areas where visibility is poor?

36 *Drugs:* the Code gives clear advice about driving when under the influence of *drugs or medicines*. What is this advice?

***37** *Signs:* describe the sign meaning *'no stopping (clearway)'.*

38 *Lanes:* on some dual carriageways each carriageway has *three lanes;* what should each lane be used for?

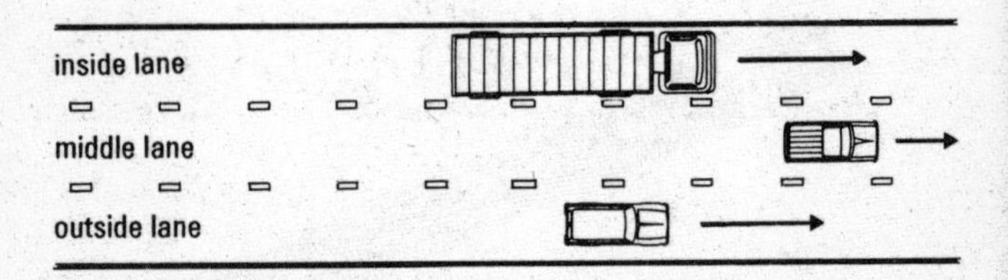

39 *Traffic lights:* under what circumstances would you *not* go forward when the lights are green?

40 *Motorway procedure:* what do you do if you accidentally drive past your turn-off point?

41 *Lanes:* what is the meaning of white, red, amber and green *reflecting road studs*?

42 *Cyclists:* describe how a cyclist would make a safe right turn.

43 *Turning right:* describe the procedure for making a *right turn*.

44 *Lanes:* under what circumstances may you use the lanes on the *right-hand* half of a four-lane single carriageway road?

45 *Signs:* what are the meanings of these three similar signs, all of which are in red triangles?

46 *Cycle lanes:* these lanes are shown by signs and by solid or broken white lines. What is the significance of the *solid* white line?

47 *Signals:* what light signal does a driver use to indicate that he intends to stop on the *left*?

***48** *Riding at night:* what advice does the Code give to horse riders using the roads at night?

***49** *Stopping distances:* referring to driving on the open road, in good conditions, the Code gives a rough rule-of-thumb guide to the *minimum space* you could leave between yourself and the car in front. What is it?

50 *Horn:* you are not allowed to use your horn at *certain times and places*. What are they?

51 *Traffic lights: where* should vehicles required to stop wait at a traffic light?

***52** *Horse riding:* the Code lists three places where you may not ride your horse. What are they?

53 *Motorway lanes:* how should you approach a junction where you plan to turn off?

54 *Lines:* where there are double white lines along the middle of the road, may you overtake if the *nearer one is broken*?

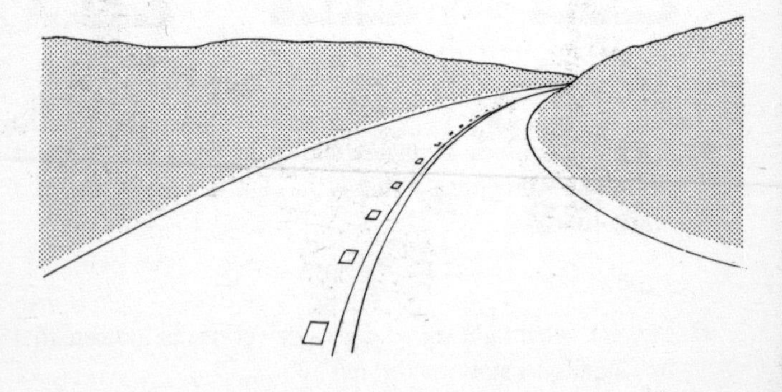

55 *Signs:* what does the sign comprising a white disc bordered by a red circle mean?

***56** *Seat belts:* what does the Code say about the driver's responsibility regarding seat belts and *children*?

***57** *Parking:* which way should your car face when you park it at night?

***58** *Signs:* describe the road sign meaning *'No overtaking'*.

***59** *Speed limits:* what are the speed limits for cars on the following types of road:
(a) roads in *built-up* areas;
(b) *single* carriageways;
(c) *dual* carriageways;
(d) *motorways*?

60 *Signals:* what are the meanings of these three arm signals?

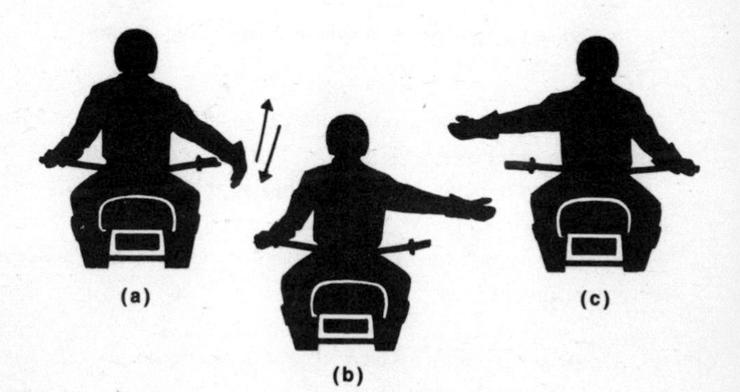

***61** *Motorway overtaking:* describe the procedure for *overtaking* on a motorway.

***62** *Level crossings:* what must you NOT do at an automatic *half-barrier* level crossing?

63 *Tinted windows:* the Code gives clear advice about *tinted windows* in your car – what is it?

***64** *Roundabouts:* you are approaching a roundabout: who should normally *give way*, you, or the traffic on your right as you enter the roundabout?

65 *Direction signs:* what does this sign tell you about the road straight ahead?

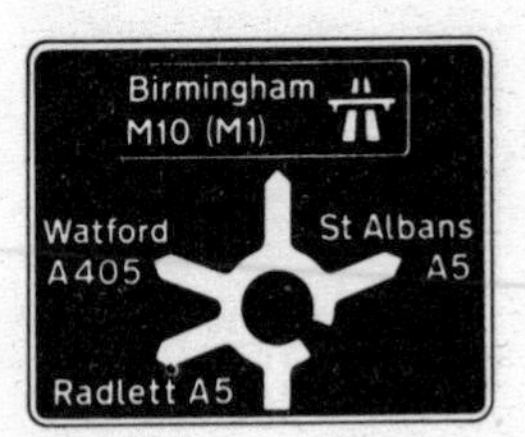

(green background, with blue rectangle at top of sign)

66 *Motorcyclists:* the Code draws a distinction between the effectiveness of *reflective* and *fluorescent* materials in helping others to see you. What is this distinction?

67 *Signals:* describe the *arm signal* given by a driver intending *to stop*.

68 *Motorway signals:* where might you *encounter this sign* and what is its meaning?

69 *One-way streets:* if you travel along a three-lane *one-way street* with no road markings, and you wish to go *straight on*, which lane should you choose:
(a) the left-hand lane;
(b) the middle lane;
(c) the right-hand lane; or
(d) the most appropriate lane?

70 *Overtaking:* describe the procedure stated in the Highway Code *for overtaking* in a car.

71 *Reversing:* if you can't see clearly behind, what does the Code say you should do?

72 *Junctions:* what is the procedure for *driving across a dual carriageway?*

***73** *Driving in snow:* what does the Code say about driving in snow?

***74** *Seat belts:* who must, by law, wear a seat belt?

75 *Police signals:* what do these police signals mean?

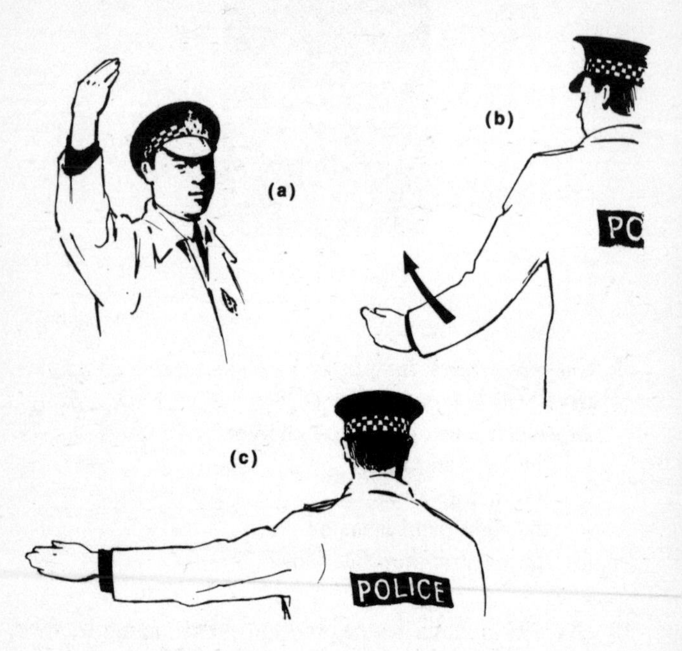

76 *Motorway procedure:* you plan to go north: you join a motorway by a slip road, and you suddenly realise you are on the *south*-bound lane; what should you do?

77 *Level crossings:* if you came across a level crossing with *lights* and *gates* but *no* attendant, how would you negotiate it?

***78** *Flashing headlights:* there is only *one* meaning, advised by the Code, for flashing your headlights; what is it?

79 *Turning left:* what particular precautions should you take if intending to turn left across a bus lane or cycle lane or a tramway on your left?

80 *Signs:* what are the meanings of these five signs?

(a)

(b)

(c)

(d)

(e)

(black figures in red triangles)

81 *Fog lights:* the Code states that you *must not* use your fog lights unless visibility is *seriously* reduced. What does 'seriously' mean?

***82** *Traffic lights:* what do the following colours of traffic lights indicate:

- Red and amber?
- Green?
- Amber only?
- Red only?

83 *Motorway signals:* what do you do if you encounter *flashing red lights* above your lane on a motorway?

84 *Overtaking:* when does the 'overtake on the right' rule not apply (4 points)?

85 *Turning left:* describe how you would execute a *left-hand* turn.

***86** *Alcohol:* the Highway Code gives *four* specific examples of how driving ability may be seriously affected by alcohol. Please state what these are.

87 *Direction signs:* what does a *green background*, found on many signs, indicate?

88 *Manoeuvres:* what definite *procedures* does the Code say you should carry out *well before* you overtake, turn, change lane, change speed or stop?

89 *Motorway overtaking:* in what circumstances may you use the hard shoulder for overtaking?

90 *Accidents:* how would you *adjust your driving* if you suspected that there was an accident ahead?

91 *Stopping distances:* what is the overall stopping distance for a car travelling at *40 m.p.h.?* (Answer in *metres* or *feet*.)

***92** *Accidents:* if something *falls from your vehicle,* what would you do about it:
(a) on an ordinary road;
(b) on a motorway?

93 *Signs:* what is the meaning of this sign?

(white flashes on blue background)

94 *Speed limits:* give the speed limits for a car *towing* a caravan in the following situations:

(a) in a *built-up* area;
(b) on a *single* carriageway;
(c) on a *dual* carriageway;
(d) on a *motorway.*

95 *Signals:* what is the meaning of *these flashing indicators?*

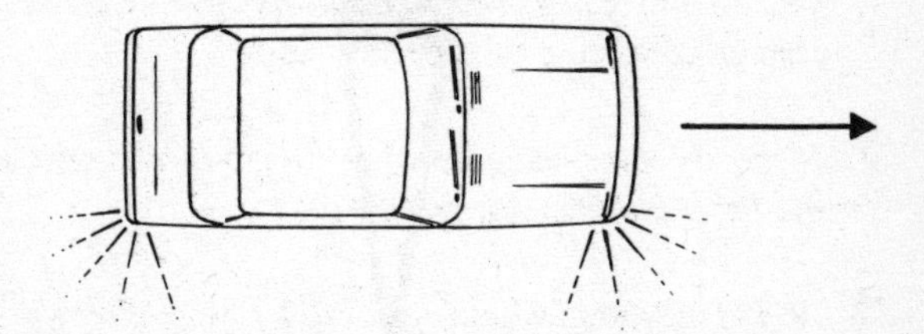

***96** *Seat belts:* can a very young child travel in the front passenger seat simply wearing a seat belt?

97 *Level crossings:* what is an open level crossing, and what should you do if you come to one?

98 *Lights:* what should you do, if when driving, you are *dazzled by approaching headlamps?*

***99** *Box junctions:* what is the rule about entering *box junctions* when you want to *turn right*?

100 *Signs:* what are the meanings of these two signs?

(in (a) white letter on green, yellow border (b) black letters, yellow background, black border)

101 *Pedestrians:* certain pedestrians, especially when crossing the road, require more consideration from drivers than others; who are they?

102 *Road markings:* what does this white marking mean?

***103** *Motorway breakdown:* what advice does the Code give you should your car happen to *break down* on the motorway? (It is assumed that you can get your car on to the hard shoulder. There are eleven main points).

104 *One-way streets:* you are driving along a three-lane *one-way street*, and you wish to turn *right*: which lane should you be in:

(a) the left-hand lane;

(b) the right-hand lane; or
(c) the middle lane?

105 *Lane changing:* in slow-moving traffic queues the Code advises that you may change lanes to the left for *one* reason only. What is it?

106 *Signs:* what is the meaning of this sign?

(white sign on blue background)

107 *Loads:* what three points does the Code mention with regard to any *load* you may tow or carry?

***108** *Green filters:* what must you remember when you come across traffic lights which have a *green arrow filter* indicating a filter-only lane?

109 *Motorways:* may you, under normal circumstances, *walk* on the carriageway of a motorway?

110 *Level crossings:* you are waiting at an automatic level crossing, a train has gone by, but the lights continue to flash and the barriers stay down. What does this mean?

***111** *Flashing headlights:* if you want to overtake someone who seems not to know you are there, does the Code sanction your use of flashing headlights to let him know you are there?

112 *Roundabouts:* you are approaching a roundabout and wish to go *straight on*:

(*a*) in which lane (left or right) should you normally *approach* the roundabout?

(*b*) at which point should you use your left turn *indicator*?

(*c*) in which lane should you normally keep while *on the* roundabout?

(*d*) which lane should you use if there are more than three lanes?

113 *Junctions:* how would you negotiate a road junction where there is a *double broken white line* across the road you are in?

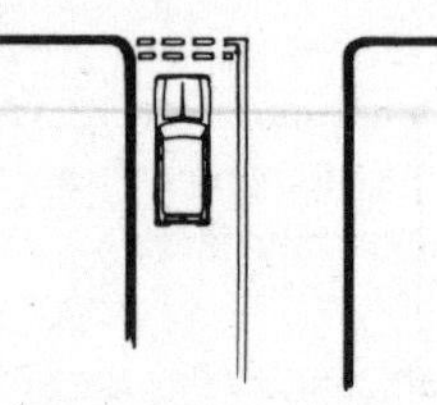

114 *Signs:* what are the meanings of these signs?

(black pictures, red triangles)

***115** *Speed rule:* what supremely important piece of advice does the Code give regarding your *speed* and the distance you can see to be *clear*?

116 *Signals:* describe the *arm signal* you would give a policeman controlling traffic if you wanted to *turn right.*

***117** *Reserved parking:* some spaces are reserved for specific users, such as Orange Badge holders or residents. Can anyone use them if they are free?

118 *Hazard lights:* if your car is fitted with a *hazard warning device* (allowing all the direction indicators to flash at the same time), under what circumstances may this be used?

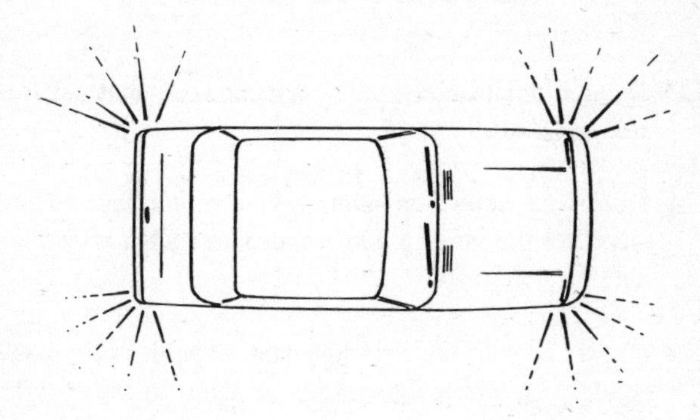

119 *Animals:* what rules of common sense should be remembered when driving past *animals*?

120 *Glasses:* if you *normally wear glasses*, should you wear them for driving?

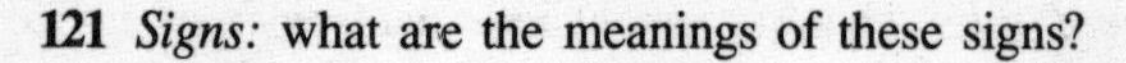

121 *Signs:* what are the meanings of these signs?

(black pictures, red triangles)

122 *Signs:* what do these two signs mean?

(white arrows on blue backgrounds)

123 *Signals:* what light signals on a car show that a driver is *slowing down*?

***124** *Motorway lanes:* on a three-lane motorway, the three lanes are the inner, middle and outer; what should each lane be used for?

***125** *Lines:* in normal driving, you should not cross or straddle *double white continuous lines* in the middle of the road; what are the exceptions to this rule?

126 *Overtaking:* when you are *being overtaken* what rules of common sense must you remember?

***127** *Junctions:* how would you negotiate a road junction which has a *'stop'* sign and an unbroken white line across the road in front of you?

128 *Direction signs:* this sign has a *yellow* background; do you know what kind of a sign it is?

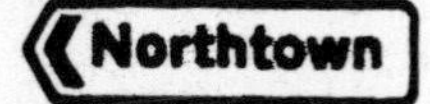

***129** *Zebra crossings:* please define the right of way rule for pedestrians at a zebra crossing.

130 *Road markings:* what is the significance of a *broken yellow line* along the edge of the road?

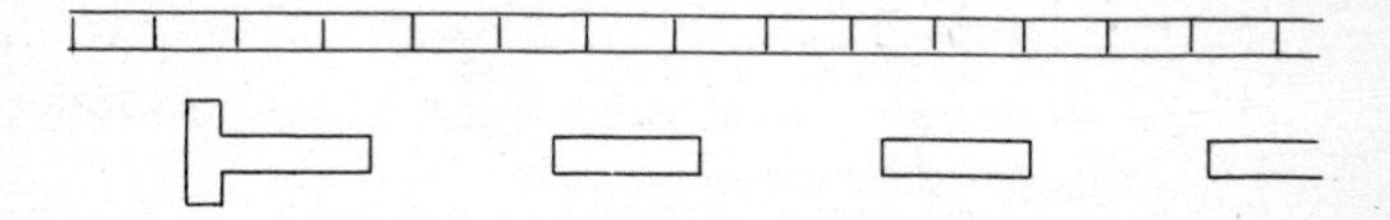

131 *Motorway parking:* where must you *not* park, under any circumstances, on a motorway?

132 *Slow vehicles:* if you are driving a slow-moving vehicle on a narrow, winding road, in what way should you give *consideration to drivers behind*?

***133** *Signals:* at pedestrian crossings, should you *signal* to pedestrians when you consider it is *safe* for them to cross?

134 *Roundabouts:* when approaching a roundabout intending to turn right, what lane should you take and what signals should you give?

135 *Estate Cars:* the Code gives clear advice about the carrying of children in the *luggage space* behind the rear seats of estate cars; what is it?

***136** *Signs:* what are the meanings of these signs?

(a) (b)

(black pictures, red triangles)

137 *Zebra crossings:* what points must drivers remember when approaching zebra crossings?

138 *Signals:* describe the arm signal for a driver intending to *turn left*.

139 *Junctions:* you are emerging from a junction, and a vehicle approaching from the right is signalling with its left-hand direction indicator. What can you or can you not assume?

***140** *Textured paving:* why do some pedestrian crossings have textured paving (usually covered with little raised dimples)?

141 *Stopping distances:* the Code publishes a table of the shortest overall stopping distances at various speeds for a good driver on dry roads, in a good car. What driving conditions could greatly increase these figures?

***142** *Motorway prohibitions:* who may *not* use the motorway? (There are eight categories.)

143 *Signs:* what is the meaning of this sign?

(background yellow; circle is red surrounding and bisecting blue centre)

144 *Seat belts:* what does the Code define as an appropriate child restraint?

***145** *Motorway procedure:* describe the procedure for *joining a motorway from a slip road,* which becomes an acceleration lane as it merges with the motorway.

146 *Single track roads:* what is a *single track road*? What should a driver going *downhill* on one particularly bear in mind?

147 *Bus and tram lanes:* at what times of day may *any vehicle use a bus or tram lane*?

148 *Signs:* what are the meanings of these signs?

(a)

(b)

(backgrounds blue except on caravan plate; small rectangle in (b) is red)

149 *Junctions:* what special consideration do you have to give to *very long vehicles* at road junctions?

150 *Road markings:* where might you expect to see a *yellow zigzag line* along the *edge* of the road?

151 *Motorway signals:* you may see *flashing amber signals;* what is their purpose, and what should be your reaction on seeing them?

152 *Overtaking:* when overtaking on a *motorway,* of what must you be especially careful?

***153** *Turning right:* describe how you would turn right from a *dual carriageway* into a side road?

***154** *Hats for horse riders:* what does the Code say about horse riders and hats?

***155** *Signs:* what do these signs mean?

(black pictures, red circles and diameters)

156 *Signals:* what is the meaning of these *flashing indicators?*

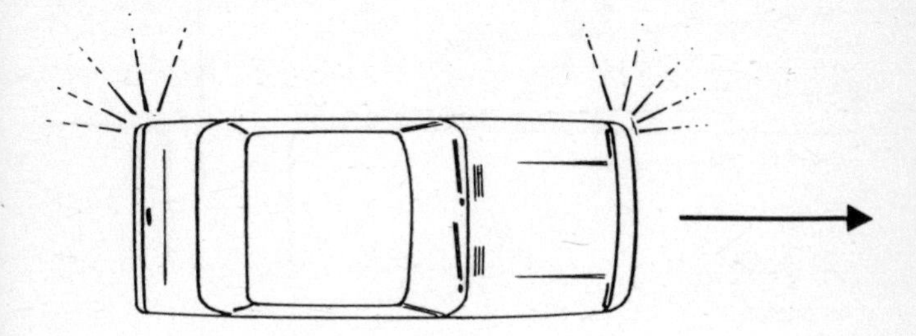

157 *Motorway overtaking:* which vehicle here is *breaking* one of the rules of the Code?

158 *Lanes:* which *rule* is being *broken* here?

159 *Overtaking:* in this situation, the Highway Code gives clear guidance as to *which car should give way;* is it A or B?

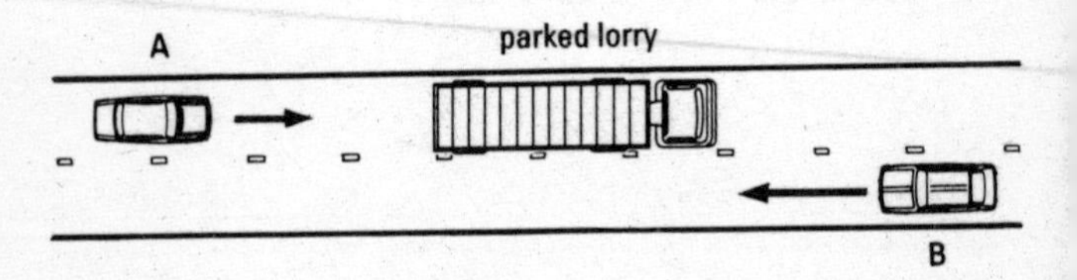

160 *Signs:* what are the meanings of these signs?

(black pictures, red triangles)

161 *Pedestrians:* name four places where it would be advisable to drive with extra caution for the benefit of pedestrians.

162 *Road markings:* what does this road marking mean and where might it be found?

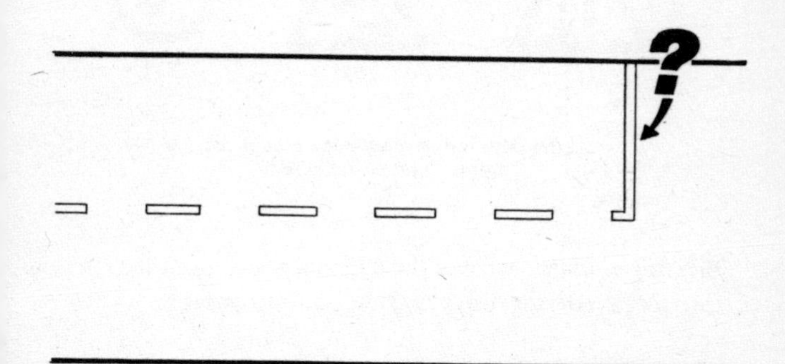

163 *Buses:* what particular consideration ought to be given to buses?

***164** *Level crossings:* what *three* things must you *never* do, when driving over any level crossing?

***165** *Police stopping procedures:* how will police in a patrol car let you know they want you to stop, and how should you respond?

166 *Horn:* other than at night, under what circumstances should you *not* sound your horn?

167 *Mini-roundabouts:*

(a) describe the sign indicating a *mini-roundabout;*

(*b*) do *rules for negotiating* a mini-roundabout differ from those for an ordinary roundabout?

168 *Signs:* what are the meanings of these signs?

(borders red, arrows black except left arrow in (c) which is red)

169 *Speed limits:* what is the national speed limit for *cars* on *single carriageways* outside built-up areas?

170 *Kerb markings:* what is the significance of *double yellow flashes* marked on the kerb?

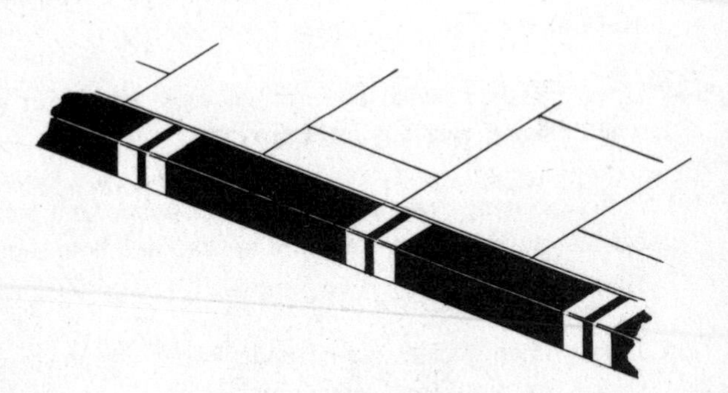

171 *Motorway signals:* what is the meaning of this sign?

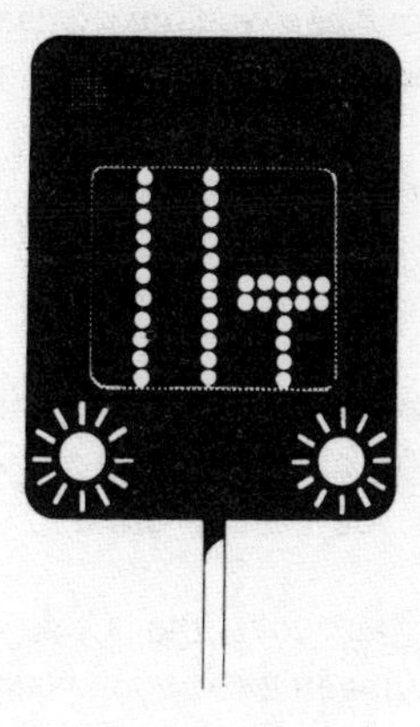

172 *Breakdowns:* how might you use an *advance warning sign* (a red reflective triangle) if your vehicle was causing an obstruction on an ordinary road?

***173** *Learner motorcyclists:* if I want to learn to ride a motorcycle, a scooter or a moped, can I just jump on and take to the road if I display L-plates?

***174** *Flashing amber lights:* what is the significance of flashing amber lights on other vehicles?

175 *Signs:* what *services* are *available* at Puddleworth?

(blue background)

*176 *Sleepiness:* how can you guard against the hazard of *sleepiness* when driving for long distances?

177 *Motorway procedure:* having just joined a motorway from a slip road, how long should you *stay in the inside lane* before moving into an overtaking lane?

178 *Single-track roads:* if you were driving along a road only wide enough for one vehicle (*a single track road*), what advice should you bear in mind?

*179 *Seat belts:* what does the Code stipulate regarding children travelling in the rear of a car *not fitted there with an appropriate child restraint?* And what is *an appropriate child restraint?*

180 *Box junctions:* describe the appearance of a *box junction* .

181 *Signs:* what do these signs mean?

(a) (b) (c) (d)

(black pictures, red borders)

182 *Signals:* describe the arm signal for a driver intending *to turn right.*

*183 *Motorway junctions:* what does the Code say you should do when approaching a junction on a motorway?

184 *Lines:* what is the purpose of areas of *white diagonal stripes* or *chevrons* which are sometimes seen on the road?

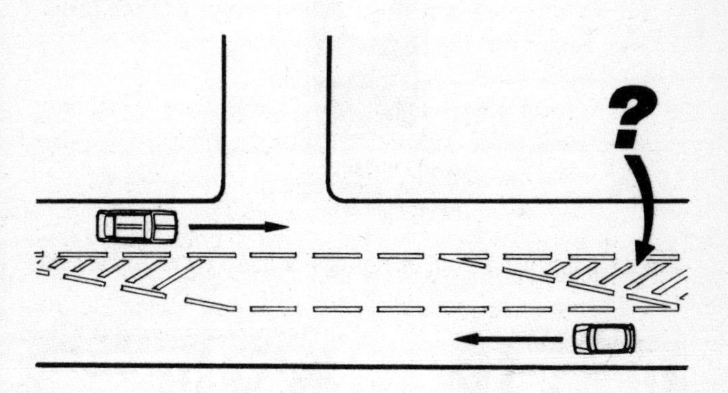

***185** *Pedestrian crossings:* what do *zigzags* mean?

***186** *Junctions:* what procedure should you normally follow when *turning right* at a junction where there is an oncoming vehicle *also* turning right?

187 *Signs:* describe the sign meaning 'Loose chippings'.

***188** *Pelican crossings:* these have a *flashing amber signal*, which follows the red signal. What does this mean?

189 *Traffic lights:* what does it mean when the traffic lights show *red* in the top light and *amber* in the middle light? (See overleaf.)

(top: red light
middle: amber light
lower light out)

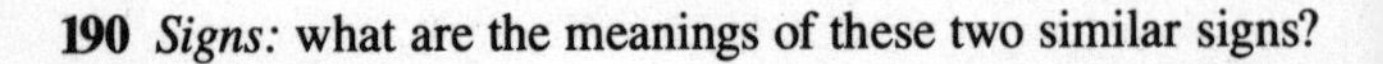

190 *Signs:* what are the meanings of these two similar signs?

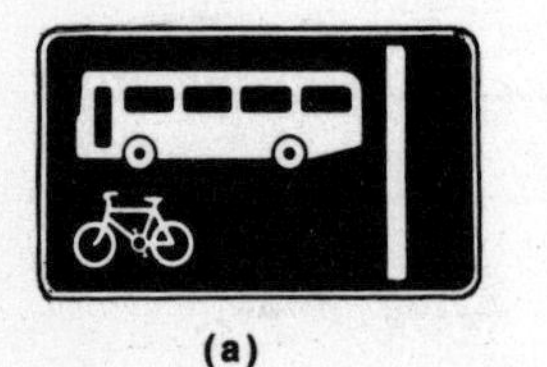

(a)

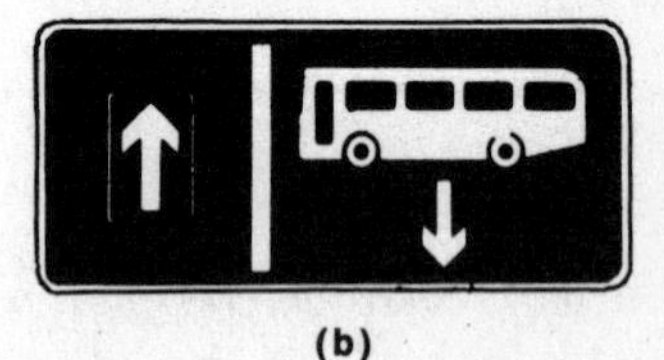

(b)

(blue backgrounds)

***191** *Horse riders:* what advice does the Code give the road user on wheels concerning horse riders apart from driving slowly and giving them plenty of room?

***192** *Traffic light failure:* what should you do if traffic lights are not working?

193 *Direction signs:* what does the *black border* on this sign signify?

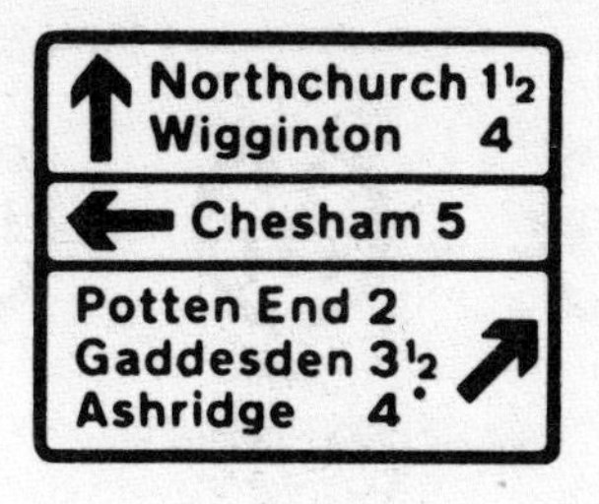

194 *Signs:* what are the meanings of these two signs, (both with red circles, but *(a)* with a white background and *(b)* with red diagonals and a blue background)?

195 *Motorway lanes:* three classes of vehicles, although they are permitted on a motorway, are normally *prohibited* from using the outside lane on a three-lane motorway. Which are these?

196 *Lanes:* what are traffic lane markings?

197 *Overtaking:* where *must* you not overtake?

198 *Dangerous goods:* what special steps should you take if you were at an accident involving a vehicle containing *dangerous goods* and displaying a hazard information panel?

199 *Signs:* what are the meanings of these signs?

(figures black, borders red)

***200** *Speed limits:* what does the presence of *street lights* on a road, other than a motorway, tell you about its speed limit?

***201** *Junctions:* what does the road marking in the drawing below mean?

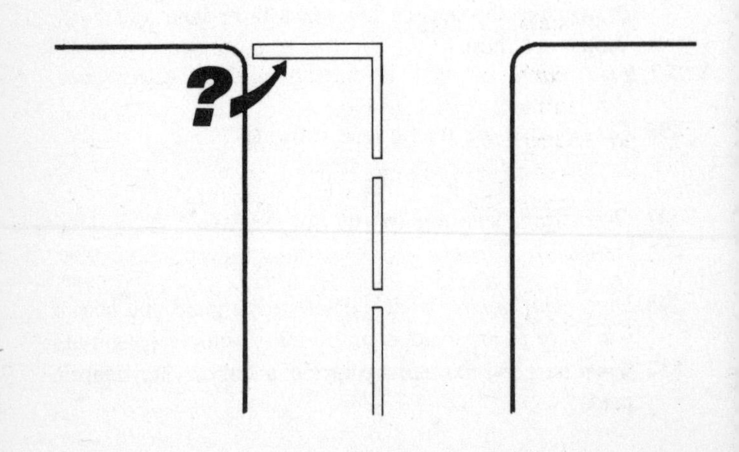

202 *Motorway cruising:* before setting out on a motorway journey, in what ways does the Highway Code say that you should ensure that your *vehicle is fit* for motorway cruising?

203 *Lights:* what daytime conditions require you to use your headlights?

***204** *Motorway procedure:* how would you turn *right* on a motorway?

205 *Signs:* what are the meanings of these signs?

(pictures black, borders red)

206 *Herding animals:* what should you do if you are herding animals along a road?

***207** *Road markings:* what is the *difference in appearance* between these road markings:
(a) a lane line;
(b) a hazard warning line; and
(c) a centre line?

208 *Motorway stopping:* you must not stop on a motorway except under two quite specific circumstances. Can you name them?

209 *Signs:* describe the sign meaning 'School crossing patrol' ahead.

***210** *Stopping distances:* what is the overall stopping distance for a car travelling at *60 m.p.h.* ? (Answer in *metres* or feet.)

211 *Reversing:* what does the Highway Code say about reversing from *a side road* into a main road?

212 *Direction signs:* what information is given by this sign?

(blue background)

***213** *Overtaking:* should you overtake on the approach to a pedestrian crossing?

214 *Signals:* what light signal does a driver use to indicate that he intends *to move out to the right?*

215 *Motorway slip roads:* what do you do if a slip road continues as an extra lane on the motorway?

216 *Signs:* what are the meanings of these two signs?

(red, amber and green lights in (a) a red triangle and in (b) a black rectangle with a red diagonal)

217 *Documents:* if, when required by the police to produce your driving licence, certificate of insurance and test certificate, and you do not have them:
(a) *where* may you produce them; and
(b) within *how many days?*

218 *Signs:* what are the meanings of these signs?

((a) with a red background, (b) with red borders)

219 *Motorway procedure:* should traffic on the motorway give way to traffic joining from a *slip road?*

220 *Broken lines:* may you cross a *single broken line* with long markings and short gaps along the middle of the road?

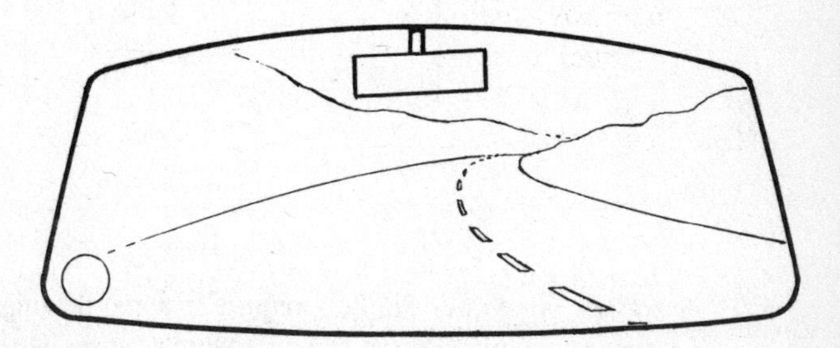

221 *Overtaking:* under what conditions of light and weather must you be *particularly careful* when overtaking?

222 *Turning right:* which of these positions is the correct one for someone wishing *to turn right?*

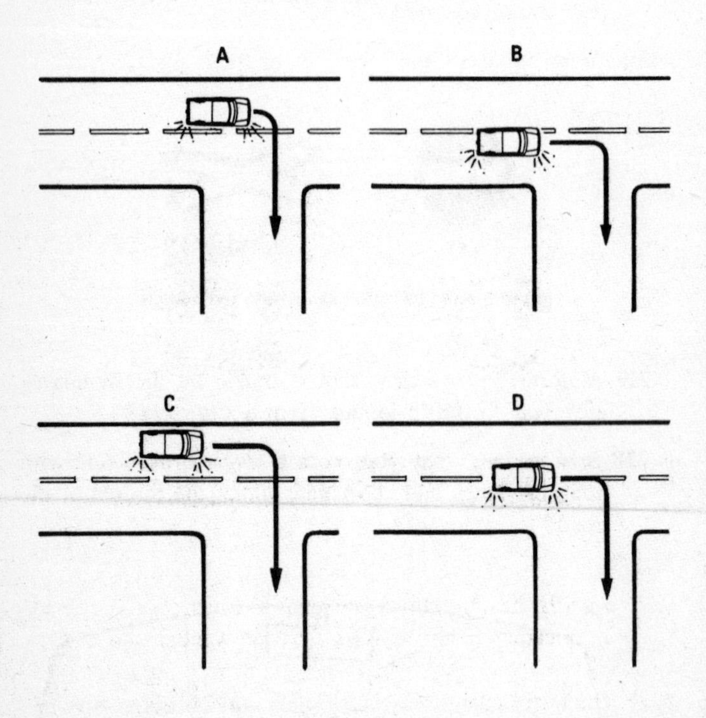

***223** *Accidents:* what does the Law require if when driving a car you are involved in an accident which causes *injury* to someone else?

224 *Signs:* what do these signs mean?

(borders red, pictures black, except right-hand car in (b) which is red)

225 *Signs:* what is the difference in meaning of these two similar signs?

((a) red circle, small red arrow points vertically upwards, large black arrow pointing downwards; (b) blue background, large white arrow pointing upwards and a smaller red arrow pointing downwards.)

226 *Signals:* describe the *arm* signal a driver should give to a policeman controlling traffic if he wanted to *turn left*.

***227** *Tramways:* the Code gives clear advice about driving where there are tramways. What are the 7 main points?

228 *Lanes:* what procedure should you follow when changing lanes?

***229** *General:* what might you expect to meet coming *towards* you on your *(left-hand)* side of a country road where there is no footpath?

***230** *Box junctions:* how should you negotiate a *box junction?*

***231** *Stopping distances:* what is the overall stopping distance for a car travelling at *70 m.p.h.?* Please express your answer in *metres* (or feet) and state how many *car lengths* this is roughly equivalent to.

***232** *Learner drivers:* the Code specifies who is allowed to accompany a learner driver. What are the criteria?

***233** *Traffic lights:* what is the meaning of these lights?

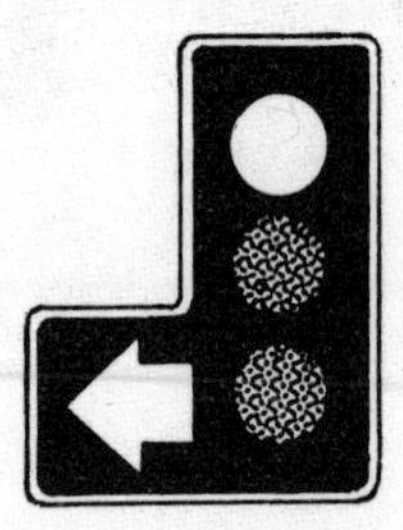

(top light red, arrow at bottom left green)

234 *Opening doors:* what precaution should you take before opening any door of your car?

235 *Breakdowns:* if you have a breakdown on the road how can you try to make sure that your vehicle does not obstruct other traffic?

236 *Signs:* describe the sign meaning *no entry.*

237 *Signs:* what are the meanings of these signs?

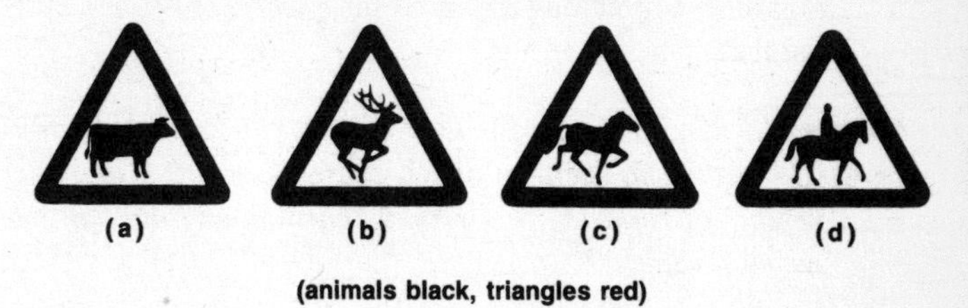

(animals black, triangles red)

238 *Pedestrians:* if you are turning at a road junction, and a pedestrian is crossing in front of you, who has the right of way?

239 *Road markings:* what is the meaning of a single yellow line along the edge of the road?

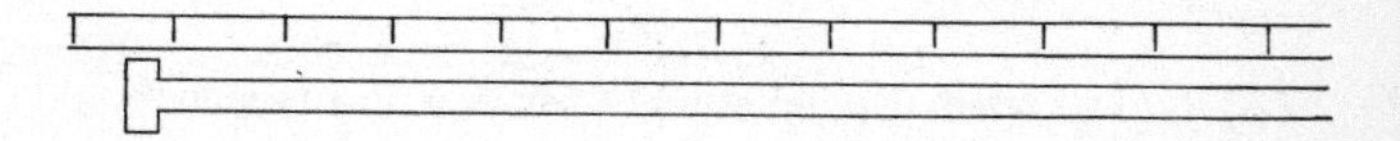

240 *Roundabouts:* some road users may have to take different courses from the usual on the approach to, and in, a roundabout. Which are they?

241 *Level crossings:* if you were unfortunate enough to break down on a crossing, what does the Code advise you to do *first*, and what does it say you should *also* do if there is time?

***242** *Junctions:* what general advice does the Code give with regard to negotiating *any* road junction? (There are four points.)

***243** *Accidents:* what does the Law require you to do if you are involved in an accident which causes *damage* to *another vehicle* or *roadside property,* or *harm* to any *animal* not in your vehicle?

***244** *Signs:* describe the sign meaning level crossing with barrier or gate.

245 *Zebra crossings:* who has the right of way at a pedestrian crossing?

246 *Motorway driving:* what general advice does the Highway Code give with regard to your speed on the motorway (4 points)?

***247** *Level crossings:* what should you do if you are driving a large or slow-moving vehicle or herding animals at a level crossing?

***248** *Lights:* when driving at night what circumstances should cause you to *dip your headlights* (3 points)?

249 *Signs:* what are the meanings of these signs?

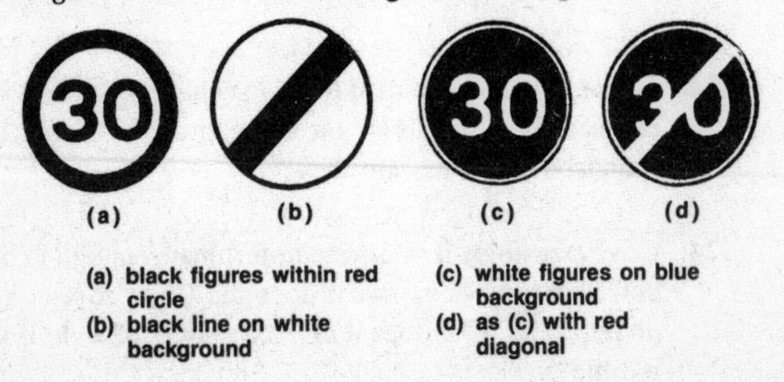

(a) black figures within red circle
(b) black line on white background
(c) white figures on blue background
(d) as (c) with red diagonal

***250** *Tyres:* what does the Law demand with regard to your car's tyres?

251 *Road markings:* what is the meaning of this white road marking?

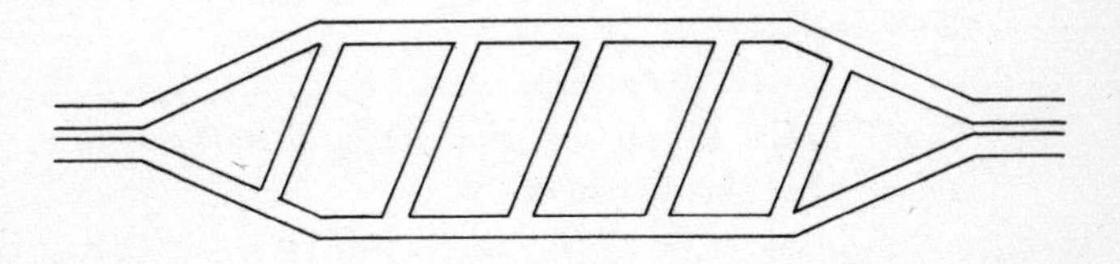

252 *Dangerous goods:* if you see a skull and crossbones on a white diamond displayed on a lorry, what does this tell you?

253 *Level crossings:* suppose you encountered a level crossing with gates, no attendant or red lights, but with a *telephone.* How does the Code advise you should negotiate this kind of crossing (seven steps)?

254 *Hazard lights:* may you drive along with all four *hazard lights* flashing?

255 *Passengers:* what does the Law require with regard to the *number* of passengers carried in your vehicle and the *manner* in which they are carried?

256 *Signs:* describe the sign meaning an *unspecified hazard.*

257 *Moving off:* what points should you remember when *moving off?*

***258** *Traffic lights:* if you are approaching a traffic light at *amber* what should you do?

(middle light amber)

***259** *Roadworks:* the Code gives specific advice on what to do when you encounter roadworks. There are seven main points. What are they?

260 *Signs and signals:* the Highway Code specifies five kinds of places where *flashing red lights* may operate. What are they and what do the flashing red lights mean?

***261** *Cyclists:* the Code gives some advice to cyclists on what they should *wear.* There are four main points: what are they?

262 *Signs:* what are the meanings of these signs?

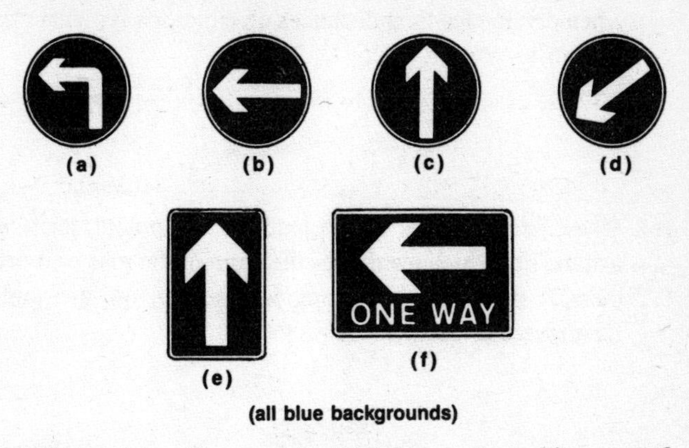

(all blue backgrounds)

263 *Road markings:* what does this road marking mean?

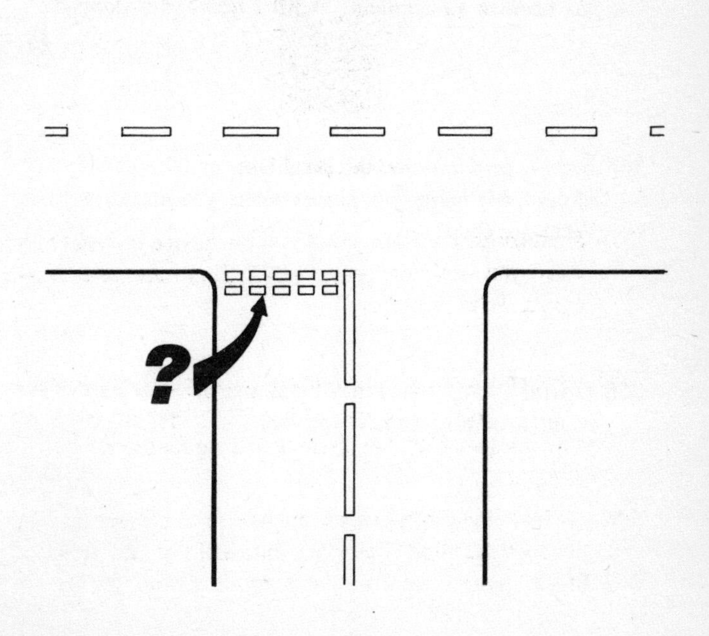

264 *Motorway sleepiness:* sleepiness is a special hazard when driving for long distances on a motorway; what can you do to prevent it?

265 *Signs:* heavy lorries with a load, or equipment, such as a crane jib, which overhangs the front or the rear by more than 2 metres, have a *special marker* on the end. Describe this marker.

266 *First aid:* what does the Code tell you to do if someone has been in an accident, and *breathing has stopped?*

267 *Driving prohibitions:* the Road User and the Law section of the Code names six places where you must not drive. What are they?

268 *Driving along:* when driving along, on *what part of the road,* generally, should you be?

269 *Police signals:* what do these *police signals* mean?

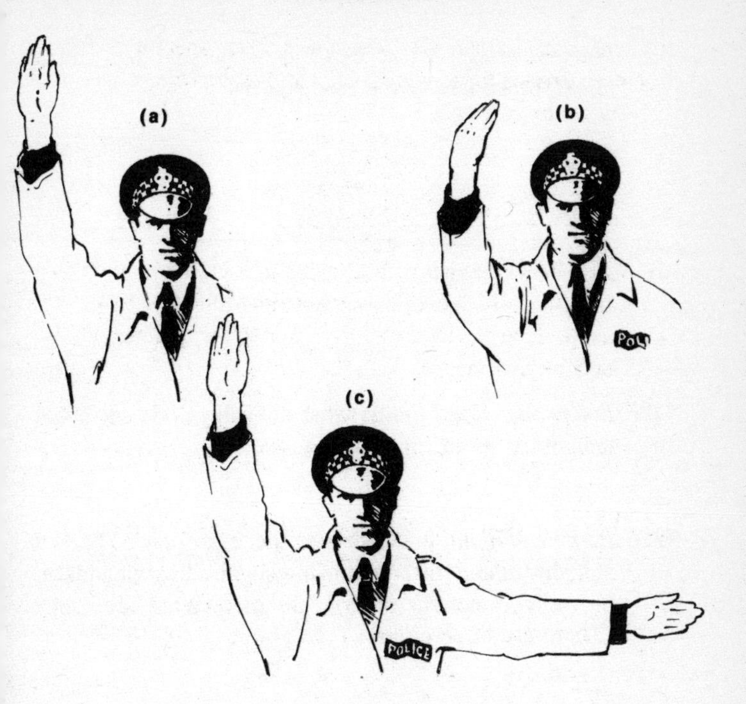

***270** *Motorway procedure:* describe the procedure for leaving a motorway by a slip road on the left.

271 *Insurance:* what does the Law require with regard to the *insurance* on your vehicle?

272 *Signs:* describe the sign meaning *all motor vehicles prohibited.*

273 *Schools:* what advice in the Highway Code must you remember when *driving past a school?*

***274** *Road markings:* what does this white marking, found along the middle of the road, mean?

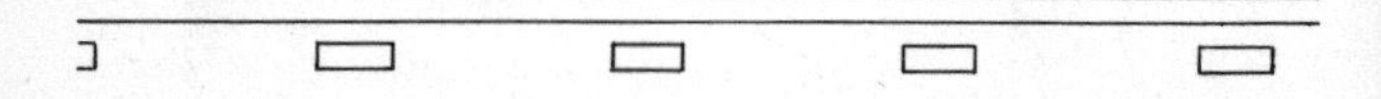

***275** *Roadworks speed limits:* what does the Code say about temporary speed limits at roadworks?

***276** *Parking at night:* the Code says that a car may be parked at night *without lights,* not in a recognised parking place, but only if certain criteria are met. What are they? (There are three criteria.)

***277** *Overtaking:* if a driver ahead signals that he intends to turn right, may you overtake *on the left?*

278 *Lights:* when should you use sidelights and headlights?

279 *Roundabouts:* what is the *correct procedure* for approaching and using a roundabout which is more than three lanes wide at its entrance?

280 *Road markings:* what is the significance of *double yellow lines* along the edge of the road?

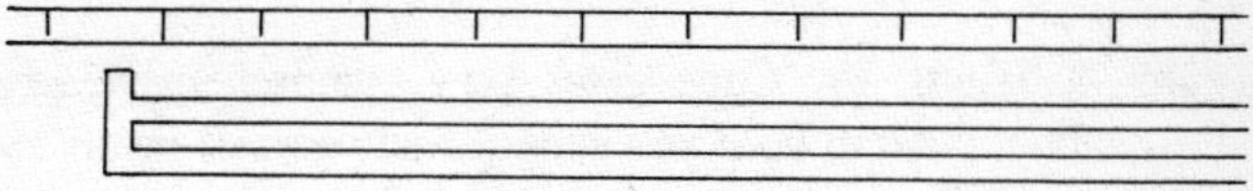

281 *Pedestrians:* what precautions should a driver take if pedestrians are walking in the road, particularly on narrow country roads (3 points)?

282 *Parking on road:* what *five things* does the Highway Code state must be done before you leave your parked car?

***283** *Motorway breakdown:*

(a) how can you quickly find out the location of the nearest *emergency telephone?*

(b) may you cross the carriageway on foot to use a nearer phone?

***284** *Fog:* what front lights should you use in *bad* fog in daytime?

285 *Reversing:* what precautions must you take *before* reversing?

***286** *Fog:* the Code gives clear advice on what to do when driving in fog. What are the main rules?

287 *Signs:* describe the sign giving advance warning of a *level crossing without gate or barrier.*

288 *Motorcyclists:* what does the Highway Code have to say about the wearing of *safety helmets, and by whom?*

***289** *Accidents:* the Code gives very comprehensive advice about what to do if you should find yourself involved in, or having stopped to give assistance at, an accident. What is the advice? (There are eight main points).

290 *Motorway procedure:* when leaving the motorway and joining ordinary traffic again what is the special significance of your speedometer?

291 *Breakdown:* how might you use *an advance warning* sign (a red reflecting triangle) if your vehicle was causing an obstruction on a motorway?

292 *Motorcyclists:* what *four* points does the Code mention about the carrying of *passengers* on a two-wheeled motorbike?

***293** *Parking:* what are a 'clearway' and an 'urban clearway'?

294 *Documents:* what four *documents* does the Law demand that you have before driving your three-year-old car?

295 *Driving along:* whereabouts on the road should you position yourself:
(a) when *driving* along normally;
(b) when *turning right* on a normal road?

***296** *Cyclists:* may I ride my bicycle along the pavement?

***297** *Crawler lanes:* where might you find a crawler lane, and what is it?

298 *Seat belts:* the Code gives two examples of people who are exempt from the seat belt law. Who are they?

299 *Dual carriageways:* on an ordinary two-lane dual carriageway, what should the right-hand lane be used for?

300 *Motorcyclists:* what special consideration should the driver always give to cyclists and motorcyclists?

Answers

1 *Accidents:* the following may forewarn you of an accident ahead:

(a) several vehicles in the distance moving *slowly* or having stopped;

(b) accident *warning signs*, hazard warning lights, or red triangles;

(c) police and emergency vehicles using *flashing lights.*

(rules 150 and 152)

***2** *Stopping distances:* for a good car with an alert driver on a dry road, the overall stopping distance for a car going at 50 m.p.h. is *53 metres* (175 feet), roughly equal to *thirteen* car lengths.

(rule 57)

3 *Roundabouts:* unless there are signs or road markings indicating otherwise, approach the roundabout in the left-hand lane and keep to that lane in the roundabout. Use the left turn indicator on approach and through the roundabout. Where there are *more* than three lanes, use the most appropriate.

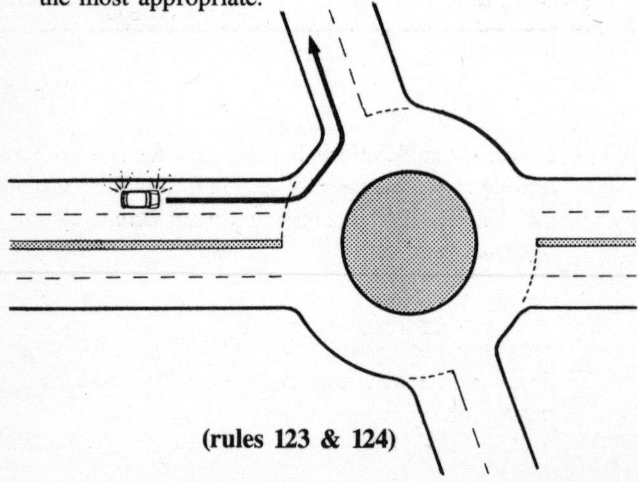

(rules 123 & 124)

4 *Signals:* the arm signal meaning that you want to go straight on is left hand held up, palm forwards.

5 *Motorway lanes:* on a motorway with a two-lane carriageway, drive in the left-hand lane except when overtaking.

hard shoulder
driving lane
overtaking lane

(rule 164)

6 *Lanes:* the middle lane is used only for *overtaking* and *turning right*. 'Remember – you have no more right to use the middle lane than a driver coming from the opposite direction'.

(rule 92)

7 *Motorway prohibitions:* 'You MUST NOT pick up or set down anyone on a slip road or on any other part of a motorway'.

(rule 181)

8 *Lights:* you must make sure that the lamps are clean, that they work, and that the headlamps are properly adjusted. 'Badly adjusted headlights can dazzle other road users and may cause accidents.'

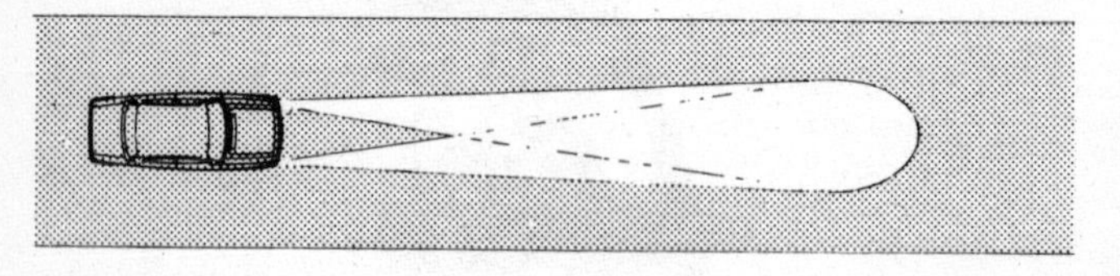

(rule 131)

9 *Signs:* bus lane on road at junction ahead.

10 *Vehicle condition:* the Highway Code advises that particular attention be paid to lights, brakes, steering, tyres (including spare), exhaust system, seat belts, demisters, windscreen wipers and washers. It also advises you to keep windscreens, windows, lights, indicators, reflectors, mirrors and number plates clean and clear. **(rule 28)**

***11** *Traffic lights:* the sequence of colours on traffic lights is:
(a) red;
(b) red and amber;
(c) green;
(d) amber;
(e) red.

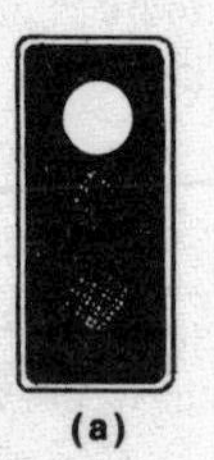
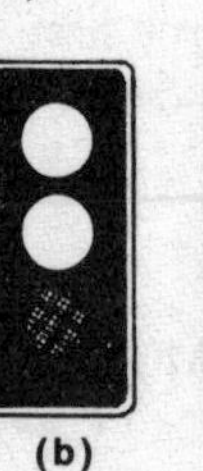
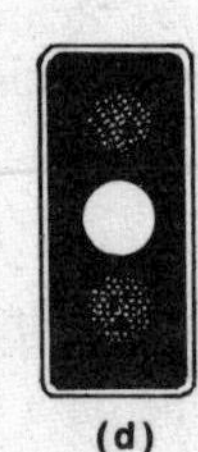
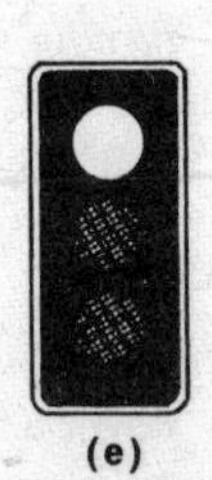

(a) (b) (c) (d) (e)

(rule 114)

***12** *Motorway overtaking:* yes, when traffic is moving in queues and the traffic queue on your right is moving more slowly than you are. **(rule 167)**

***13** *Stopping distances:* the overall stopping distance at 30 m.p.h. is *23 metres* (75 feet) which is roughly equivalent to *six* car lengths. **(rule 57)**

***14** *Pelican crossings:* the pedestrian signals for a *puffin crossing* are on your side of the road, not opposite as in a *pelican crossing*. You may cross only when a green man signal is lit, NOT when a red man is showing. Infra-red detectors vary the length of time to allow pedestrians to cross safely. **(rule 16)**

15 *Signs:*
(a) cycles only;
(b) with-flow cycle lane;
(c) no cycling;
(d) cycle route ahead;
(e) recommended route for cycles.

16 *Ice-cream vans:* drive carefully and be especially watchful for *children.* **(rule 67)**

17 *Kerb markings:* triple yellow flashes on the kerb mean no loading or unloading during every working day and additional times, as shown on nearby plates.

18 *Motorway procedure:* a motorway is a special dual carriageway road from which certain road users are excluded. **(rule 155)**

***19** *Lines:* if the nearer one is continuous, *do not cross or* *straddle it*, but if it is broken, you *may* cross if safe, and provided that you have time to cross back again before reaching a continuous white line on your side.

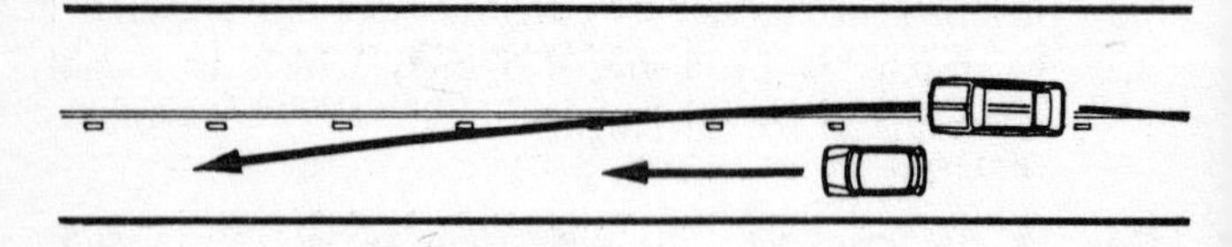

(rules 84 & 85)

20 *Motorcyclists:* the Code says you should also wear '*eye protectors*, and strong *boots, gloves* and *clothes* that will help protect you if you fall off'. The Code recommends that you also wear something *light coloured* or *bright*. Use fluorescent materials by day, but reflective ones at night. **(rule 30)**

21 *Tiredness:* the Code says 'If you feel tired or ill, DO NOT DRIVE.' **(rule 31)**

22 *Signs:* the quayside or river bank sign is a red triangle enclosing a car toppling off an edge into some water.

23 *Car telephones:* the Code tells you *not* to use a telephone handset while you are *moving*, and *not* to stop on a *motorway* to make or take a call, except in an emergency; you must not use a hands-free microphone if it distracts you. **(rule 43)**

24 *Signals:*

(a) the driver intends to *move in to the left* or *turn left;*
(b) the driver intends to *slow down* or *stop;*

(c) the driver intends to *move out to the right* or *turn right.*

*25 *Parking:* places where – and in some cases near where – you must not stop or park are as follows:

● any part of a motorway, except in a traffic queue, an emergency, or when instructed to do so by police, motorway signals or emergency signs;

● a pedestrian crossing;

● the area at a pedestrian crossing marked by zigzag lines (see rule 72);

● a clearway;

● an urban clearway within its hours of operation, except to pick up or set down passengers;

● a road marked with double white lines, even if one of the lines is broken, except to pick up or set down passengers;

● a bus, tram or cycle lane during its time of operation;

● where there are parking restrictions shown by yellow lines along the edge of the road, or by red lines on specially designated red routes;

● on a footpath;

● on a cycle track;

● at or near a bus stop;

● on a pavement;

● near school entrances;

● at or near a taxi rank;

● on the approach to a level crossing;

● within 10 metres of a junction, except in an authorized parking space;

● near the brow of a hill;

● near a hump bridge;

● opposite a traffic island;

● opposite another parked vehicle if to do so would cause an obstruction;

● where you would force other traffic to enter a tram lane;

- where the kerb has been lowered to help wheelchair users;
- in front of the entrances to property;
- in a parking space reserved for specific users, such as orange badge holders or residents, unless authorised to do so;
- if parking at night, facing *against* the direction of the traffic flow on your side;
- and in general *anywhere 'where it would endanger or inconvenience pedestrians or other road users'.*

(rules 138, 139, 140, 141, 142, 179 and 180)

26 *Junctions:* the Code says that you should *look out for* cyclists and pedestrians *before* you turn. **(rule 107)**

*27 *Stopping distances:* for a good car with an alert driver on dry roads doing 20 m.p.h. the overall stopping distance is *12 metres* (40 feet). **(rule 57)**

28 *Horn:* you should sound your horn only to let others know you are there; 'never sound your horn aggressively'. **(rule 136)**

29 *Sun-glasses:* 'at night or in poor visibility do not use tinted glasses, lenses or visors'. **(rule 35)**

30 *Pedestrians:* a deaf/blind person might carry a white stick with two red reflective bands. **(rule 64)**

*31 *Winter driving:*

- Make sure that your car's battery is well maintained;
- The radiator and windscreen washer bottle should have the correct anti-freeze in them;
- Drive with great care in freezing or near freezing conditions – even if the roads have been gritted;
- 'Take care when overtaking gritting vehicles,

particularly if you are riding a motorcycle;

- Don't drive in snow unless you absolutely must.

(rules 59, 60 & 61)

32 *Kerb markings:* single yellow flashes indicate a restriction on loading or unloading for periods not covered by double or triple yellow chevrons, as explained by the plates nearby.

***33** *Motorway lanes:* overtaking; on a three-lane motorway, the outside lane should be used only for overtaking traffic in the middle lane. 'You may use the lane to the right of a stream of slower vehicles to overtake them, but return to the lane to your left when you have passed them'. **(rule 164)**

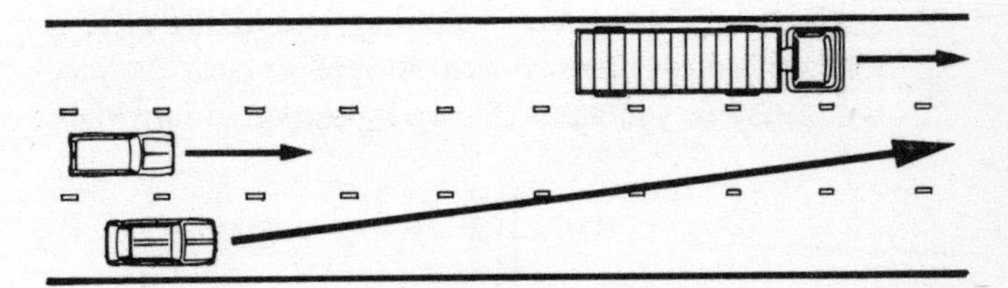

34 *Overtaking:* when overtaking motorcycles, pedal cycles or horse riders *'give them at least as much room as you would give a car'.* **(rule 101)**

35 *Lights:*

(*a*) headlights;
(*b*) headlights or front fog lamps;
(*c*) the rule is that you must switch on your sidelights at sunset;
(*d*) dipped headlights. **(rules 131 & 132)**

36 *Drugs:* the Code states that you 'MUST NOT drive under the influence of drugs or medicines'. If you are taking

medicines, check with your doctor or a pharmacist.
(rule 33)

***37** *Signs:* no stopping (clearway) sign is a *blue disc* with a *red border* and two red *diagonal stripes*, crossing in the middle.

38 *Lanes:* 'On a three-lane dual carriageway, stay in the left-hand lane. If there are slower vehicles than you in that lane, use the middle lane to overtake them but return to the left-hand lane when it is clear. The right-hand lane is for overtaking (or turning right); if you use it for overtaking, move back into the middle lane and then into the left-hand lane as soon as it is safe to do so'. The Code emphasises that you must not stay in the middle lane if you can return to the left-hand lane. **(rule 95)**

39 *Traffic lights:* when green is showing, you MUST NOT go forward 'unless there is room for you to clear the junction safely or you are taking up a position to turn right'.

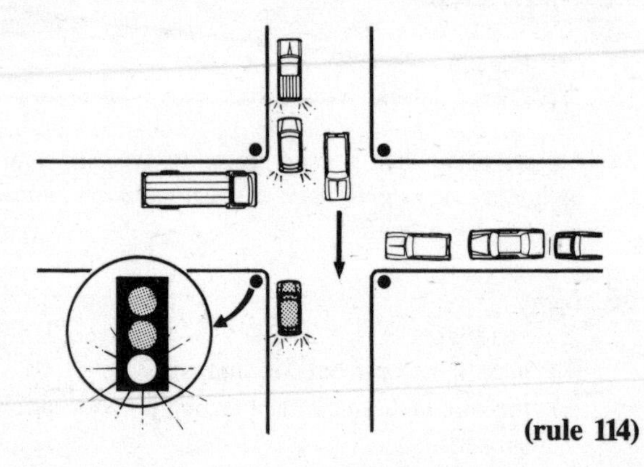

(rule 114)

40 *Motorway procedure:* you must carry on until you reach the next exit; you must not reverse, turn back or attempt to cross the central reservation. **(rule 163)**

41 *Lanes: white studs* may mark the middle of a single carriageway road or any *other* lane divisions it may have. On motorways and dual carriageways however, they only define the lanes; *amber studs* show the edge of the central reservation on some dual carriageways and all motorways; *green studs* are used across lay-bys and side roads on major routes, and always to mark the line between a slip road and a motorway. **(rules 87 & 174)**

42 *Cyclists:* check the traffic behind you, signal and when it is safe move to the centre of the road. Wait for a safe gap in the traffic before starting to turn. It may be safer to wait on the left, or to get off and wheel your bicycle across the road. **(rule 198)**

43 *Turning right:* well before the actual turn, check the mirrors for following traffic. Give a right-turn signal and, as soon as it is safe, position yourself just left of the middle of the road (or in the space marked for right turning traffic) trying to leave room for vehicles to pass on the left. Wait for a safe gap, look out for cyclists, motorcyclists and pedestrians, and turn without cutting the corner, giving way to any pedestrians who are crossing the road into which you are turning. Remember: *mirrors-signal-manoeuvre.*

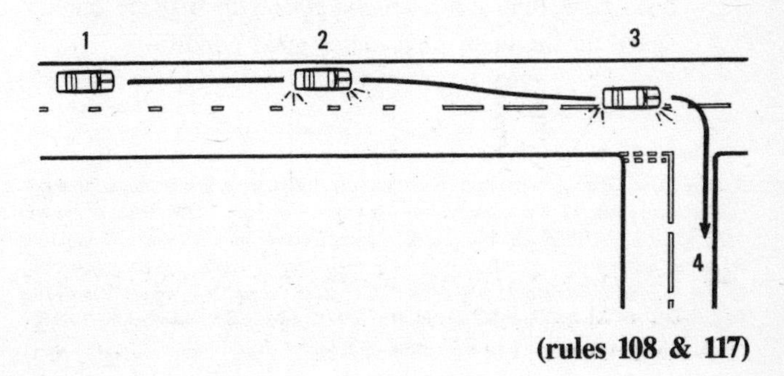

(rules 108 & 117)

44 *Lanes:* you may only use these lanes when signs and markings indicate that you are allowed to.

(rule 93)

45 *Signs:*
(a) road narrows on right;
(b) road narrows both sides;
(c) dual carriageway ends.

46 *Cycle lanes:* you MUST NOT drive or park in a cycle lane with a solid white line, during its period of operation.

(rule 98)

47 *Signals:* he uses the flashing indicator signal on the left of his car.

***48** *Riding at night:* wear reflective clothing and carry lights which show white to the front and red to the rear. The horse should have reflective bands on its legs.

(rule 219)

***49** *Stopping distances:* although the safe rule is never to get closer than the shortest stopping distances, the Code does state that a *two-second time gap* may be enough space on the open road under good conditions.[1]

(rule 57)

[1] AUTHOR'S NOTE: The above rule is probably fine, provided the car in front doesn't stop dead; if it does, you may well crash into it. Suppose, for example, you are doing 70 m.p.h. and, following rule 57, two seconds away from the car in front. In two seconds you will cover 63 metres at 70 m.p.h. The overall stopping distance for a car doing 70 m.p.h. is *96 metres* and not 63! So, if the car in front *stops dead or has an accident*, you won't be able to come to a complete stop before hitting it. In the author's humble opinion, the Department of Transport should look again at rule 57 and consider whether the 2-second rule shouldn't be replaced with a 3-second or even a 4-second one.

50 *Horn:* you must not sound your horn at night (23.30-07.00) in a built-up area. **(rule 136)**

51 *Traffic lights:* vehicles must wait *behind* the solid white 'stop' line marked across the approach. **(rule 114)**

***52** *Horse riding:* the Code says 'You MUST NOT take a horse on to a footpath, pavement or cycle track. Use a bridle-path where possible'. **(rule 222)**

53 *Motorway lanes:* make sure you are in the correct lane; remember that at some junctions a lane may lead directly off the motorway. **(rule 165)**

54 *Lines:* you *may* cross the lines to overtake *providing* it is safe to do so and that you can get back to your own side before reaching any solid white line on your side. In the illustration it is doubtful if it would be safe. **(rule 85)**

55 *Signs:* it means 'no vehicles'.

***56** *Seat belts:* the driver is responsible by *law* for ensuring that children under 14 are *suitably restrained* whether they are travelling in the *front* or the *rear.* **(rule 40)**

***57** *Parking:* at night you may park only facing the same way as the direction of the traffic flow on your side of the road. **(rule 142)**

***58** *Signs:* the 'No overtaking' sign shows a *black* car with a *red* car on its right, the two being surrounded by a red circle.

***59** *Speed limits:* unless signposted differently the maximum speed limits for cars are as follows:
- *(a)* roads in built-up areas: *30 m.p.h.*
- *(b)* *single* carriageways: *60 m.p.h.*
- *(c)* *dual* carriageways: *70 m.p.h.*
- *(d)* motorways: *70 m.p.h.* **(rule 54 and table)**

60 *Signals:* the motorcyclist intends:
- *(a)* to slow down or stop;
- *(b)* to move out to the right or turn right;
- *(c)* to move in to the left or turn left.

***61** *Motorway overtaking:*
- *(a)* use your mirrors to check that the overtaking lane is clear for a long way *behind*. Make sure it is also clear *ahead*. If you are uncertain on either score, wait;

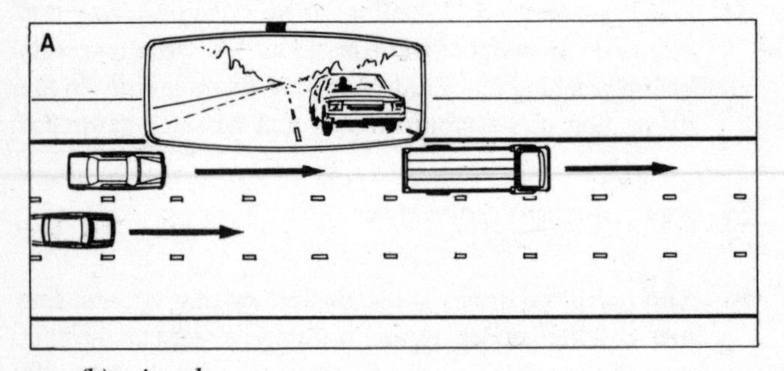

- *(b)* *signal;*

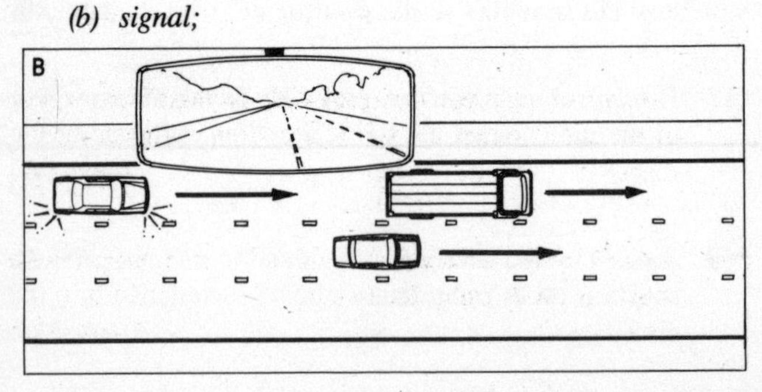

(*c*) when safe, move out and overtake; and

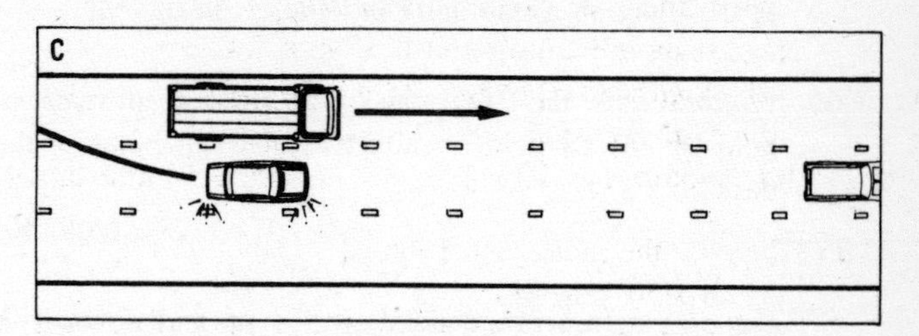

(*d*) signal your intention to move in after you overtake. Always return to the left-hand lane or, if that lane is occupied, to the middle lane as soon as you can. Never cut in.

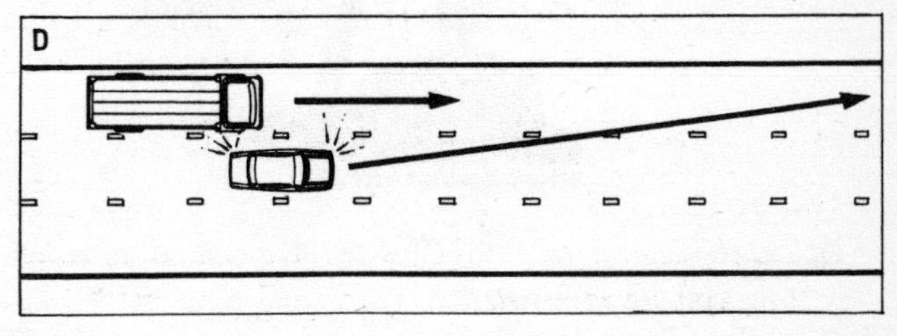

(rules 168, 169)

***62** *Level crossings:* you must NEVER zigzag around half barriers. If they are down, a train is approaching.

(rule 228)

63 *Tinted windows:* the Code says 'Do *not* use spray-on or other tinting materials for windows and windscreens'.

(rule 35)

***64** *Roundabouts:* normally *you* should give way to the traffic on your immediate right.

(rule 123)

65 *Direction signs:* it tells you that the M10 motorway *starts* at the junction ahead and that it *leads to* the M1.

66 *Motorcyclists:* the Code states that 'fluorescent material helps in the daylight… reflective material helps in the dark'.

(rule 30)

67 *Signals:* right arm extended, waved up and down with palm downwards.

68 *Motorway signals:* usually on the central reserve: it means *end of restriction.*

(rule 170)

69 *One-way streets:* in the absence of road markings, you should choose the *most appropriate lane.*

(rule 96)

70 *Overtaking:*

(a) check the road to be *clear ahead:* use your mirrors to check the road is clear *behind;*
(b) if safe, signal and move out;
(c) overtake quickly, leaving plenty of room;
(d) return to the left as soon as you can, but *without cutting in.*

Remember: *mirrors-signal-manoeuvre.*

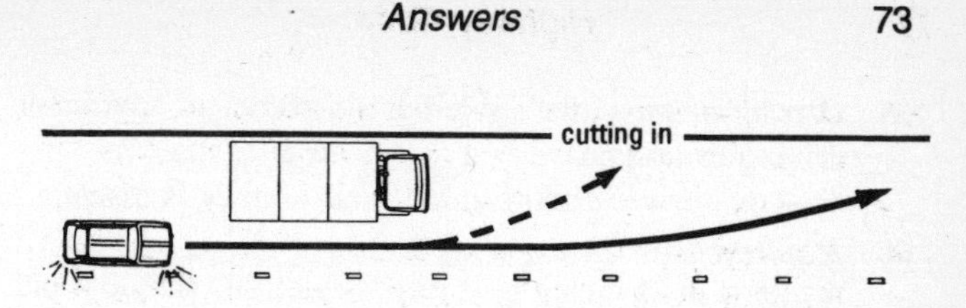

(rules 99, 100)

71 *Reversing:* the Code says you should 'get someone to guide you' when you reverse.

(rule 129)

72 *Junctions:* treat each half as a separate road. Wait in the central reservation until there is a safe gap in the traffic on the second half of the road. But if your vehicle is too long to fit in this gap, wait in the side road until you can cross the dual carriageway in one movement.

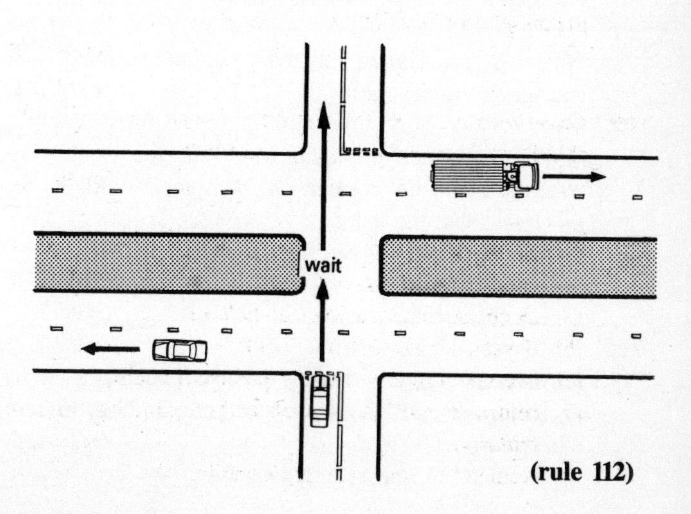

(rule 112)

*73 *Driving in snow:* the Code has six pieces of advice for driving in snow:

- Don't drive in snow unless your journey is essential;
- Drive slowly;
- Keep in as high a gear as possible; this should avoid wheel spin;
- 'Avoid harsh acceleration, steering and braking';
- 'You MUST use headlights when visibility is seriously reduced by falling snow';
- Watch out for snow ploughs, and do not overtake them unless the overtaking lane has been cleared.

(rules 61, 62 & 131)

*74 *Seat belts:* the Code states that everyone must wear a seat belt, if fitted, unless exempt. **(rule 40)**

75 *Police signals:*
(a) *come on* – to vehicles from the side;
(b) *come on* – to vehicles from behind;
(c) *stop* – to vehicles from behind.

76 *Motorway procedure:* you must continue driving until you reach the next exit. **(rule 163)**

77 *Level crossings:* if the lights were *red*, you would wait until the *green* lights came on, then you would:
(a) open *both* the gates;
(b) check that the *green light* is still showing;
(c) cross quickly;
(d) close *both* the gates. **(rule 232)**

*78 *Flashing headlights:* you may flash your headlamps to let another road user know you are there, and not for any other reason. **(rule 135)**

79 *Turning left:* give way to any vehicles, *especially cycles,* that may be in the lane you are crossing. Note that some such lanes run in a contra-flow direction. **(rule 122)**

80 *Signs:*
(a) elderly people crossing; *(b)* pedestrians in road; *(c)* pedestrian crossing; *(d)* school; *(e)* roadworks.

81 *Fog lights:* 'Seriously' means when visibility is reduced to less than 100 metres. **(rule 133)**

***82** *Traffic lights:*
- Red and amber: stop behind the stop line on the carriageway;
- Green: you may go on if the way is clear;
- Amber only: stop at the stop line unless you have already crossed it, or to pull up might cause an accident;
- Red only: stop behind the stop line on the carriageway. **(rule 114)**

83 *Motorway signals:* you must stop at the signal.

(rule 172)

84 *Overtaking:*
(a) if the driver in front is going to turn right, provided you can overtake him safely; but note that you MUST NOT do this if it means using a bus or tram lane during its working period, unless signs say you can.

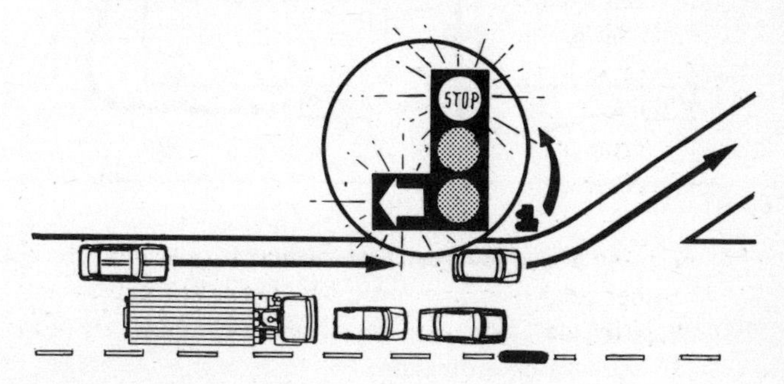

(b) when you want to turn left at a junction;
(c) in slow-moving queues where the outer lanes are moving more slowly;
(d) in a one-way street, if the lane for your destination passes to the left of lanes for other destinations.

(rules 96, 97, 102, 103)

85 *Turning left:*

(a) well before the actual turn, check your *mirrors;*
(b) give a left turn *signal;*
(c) do not overtake a cyclist, motorcyclist or horse rider just before turning left;
(d) *turn,* always checking for traffic coming up on your left and always giving way to pedestrians in the road you are about to enter.

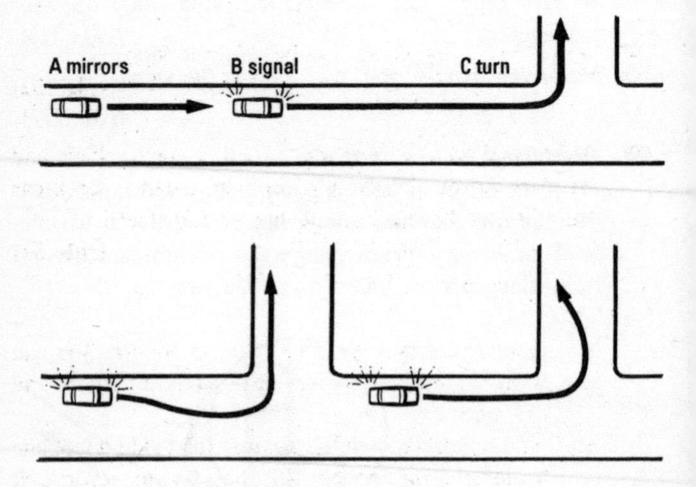

Do not swing out, before or after the turn. **(rule 121)**

***86** *Alcohol:* the Code says that drinking alcohol:

(a) reduces co-ordination;

(*b*) slows down your reactions;
(*c*) affects your judgment of speed, distance and risk; and
(*d*) gives you a false sense of confidence. **(rule 39)**

87 *Direction signs:* green backgrounds are used on signs showing *primary roads*.

88 *Manoeuvres:* well before any such manoeuvre you should:
(*a*) use your *mirrors;*
(*b*) then give the correct signal.
Motorcyclists should always *look behind* before manoeuvring. **(rules 51, 89)**

89 *Motorway overtaking:* never. **(rule 167)**

90 *Accidents:* 'Slow down and be ready to stop'. **(rule 152)**

91 *Stopping distances:* with a dry road, a good vehicle and an alert driver, the overall stopping distance for a car travelling at 40 m.p.h. is *36 metres* (120 feet). **(rule 57)**

***92** *Accidents:*
(*a*) on an ordinary road, stop, and, as soon as you can with safety, retrieve the article from the carriageway;
(*b*) on a motorway, use the nearest road-side telephone to inform the police. Do not try to retrieve it yourself. **(rules 151 & 178)**

93 *Signs:* it is the second of three countdown markers before the *exit* from a motorway; there are 200 yards to the exit.

94 *Speed limits:* the speed limits for a car towing a caravan are:

(*a*) in a *built-up* area: *30 m.p.h.;*
(*b*) on a *single* carriageway: *50 m.p.h.;*
(*c*) on a *dual* carriageway: *60 m.p.h.;*
(*d*) on a *motorway: 60 m.p.h.*

(rule 54)

95 *Signals:* the driver intends to pull out to the right or to turn right.

***96** *Seat belts:* no: a child aged under 3 must travel in a baby carrier, child seat, harness or booster seat suitable to its weight.

(rules 40 & 41)

97 *Level crossings:* an open level crossing has no gates, barriers, attendant or traffic lights, just a 'Give Way' sign. The Code says you should 'Look both ways, listen and make sure there is no train coming before you cross. Always "Give Way" to trains – they cannot stop easily!'

(rule 234)

98 *Lights:* slow down or stop.

(rule 132)

***99** *Box junctions:* 'You may enter the box when you want to turn right and are only stopped from doing so by oncoming traffic or by vehicles waiting to turn right'.

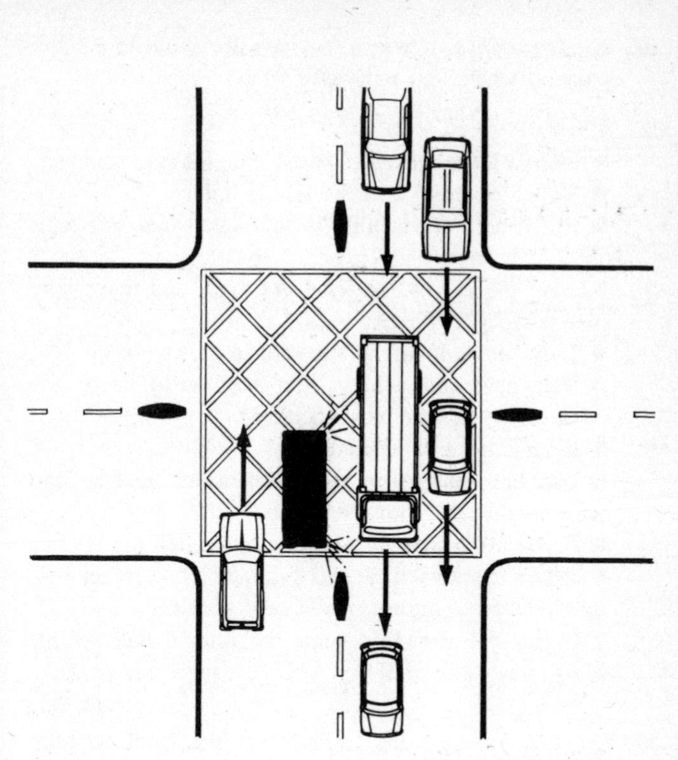

(rule 113)

100 *Signs:*

(a) ring road (primary route);
(b) holiday route.

101 *Pedestrians: children*, the *elderly*, the *blind* and *partially-sighted*, the *deaf*, and *people with other disabilities*, should be given plenty of time to cross the road. **(rule 64)**

102 *Road markings:* it warns that you are about to reach a junction where you must *give way.*

***103** *Motorway breakdown:*

- Stop *as far to the left* as possible on the hard shoulder;
- Switch on your hazard warning lights;
- If it is dark or visibility is poor, keep your *sidelights* on;
- Leave the car by the *left-hand door*, and make sure your passengers do too;
- *Leave any animals* in the vehicle.
- *Wait* near the vehicle, but well away from the carriageway and the hard shoulder;
- Keep *children* under control;
- Use the *emergency telephone,* which is free and connects directly with the police;
- If you are a *woman* travelling alone, tell the police;
- *Return* to your vehicle and wait near it but, remember, well back from the motorway/hard shoulder;
- If you feel at risk, re-enter the vehicle and *lock all doors;* stay there until you feel the danger has passed.

(rule 183)

104 *One-way streets:* the right-hand lane, unless road markings indicate differently.

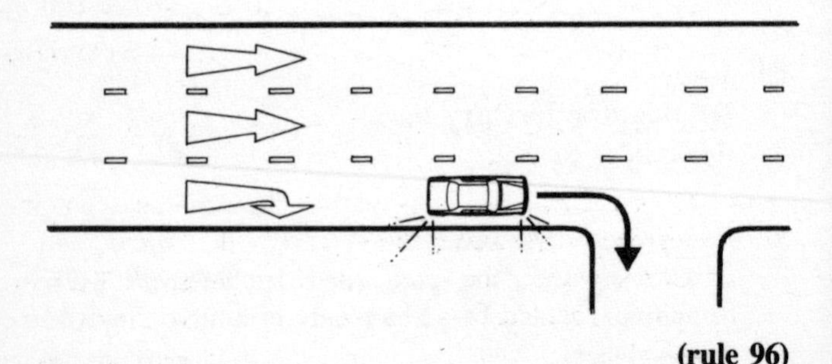

(rule 96)

105 *Lane changing:* you should only change lanes to the left in order to *turn left*. Do not change lanes to the left to overtake. **(rule 103)**

106 *Signs:* it means 'contra-flow bus lane'.

107 *Loads:* the Code says that you must ensure that any load you carry or tow:
(a) is *secure;*
(b) does not *stick out* dangerously;
(c) does not *overload* your vehicle or trailer. **(rule 29)**

***108** *Green filters:* you must not move into the filter lane unless you intend to go in the direction of the arrow. **(rule 115)**

109 *Motorways:* no, you MUST NOT walk on the carriageway except in an emergency. **(rule 182)**

110 *Level crossings:* it means that another train is coming, and that you must wait until it has passed, the lights stop flashing and the barriers open. **(rules 226, 227)**

***111** *Flashing headlights:* yes. **(rule 135)**

112 *Roundabouts:* unless signs or road markings indicate otherwise, you should:
(a) in a three-lane road, approach in the left-hand lane or the centre lane; in a two-lane road you can use the right-hand lane if the left-hand lane is blocked;
(b) you should signal left after passing the exit before the one you are taking;
(c) you should normally stay in the same lane that you approached the roundabout;
(d) where there are more than three lanes, use the most appropriate lane both on approach and through the roundabout. [Picture next page]

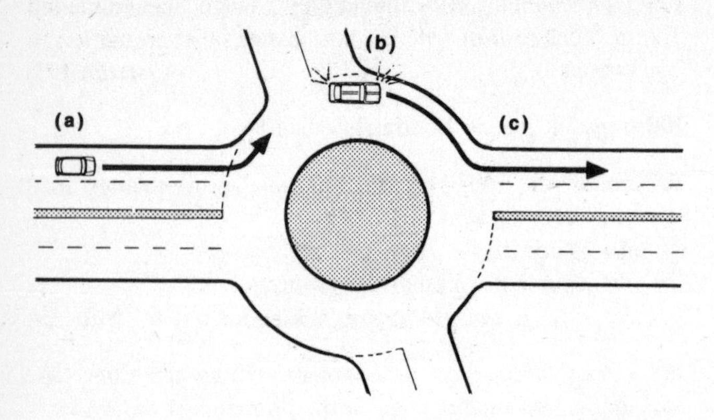

(rule 124)

113 *Junctions:* you *must* give way to traffic on the major road. Such junctions may also have 'give way' signs, or an inverted triangle on the carriageway.

(rule 110)

114 *Signs:*

(a) unspecified hazard, (plate may qualify);
(b) fallen or falling rocks.

***115** *Speed rule:* rule 57 states: *'Drive at a speed that will allow you to stop well within the distance you can see to be clear. Leave enough space between you and the vehicle in front so that you can pull up safely if it suddenly slows down or stops'.*[2]

---

[2] AUTHOR'S NOTE: in the author's opinion this rule is probably one of the most important in the entire Code, and unfortunately seems to be disregarded by many drivers. If it were universally followed there is little doubt that the carnage on the roads would be greatly reduced.

116 *Signals:* right arm fully extended out of window, palm facing forwards.

***117** *Reserved parking:* no; you MUST NOT park there.

(rule 141)

118 *Hazard lights;* a hazard warning device may be used when the vehicle is stationary to indicate that it is causing a temporary obstruction to traffic flow. While the vehicle is moving you may use hazard lights only on a motorway or unrestricted dual carriageway, and only briefly, to warn drivers behind you of a hazard or obstruction ahead.

(rule 134)

119 *Animals:* go slowly. Give plenty of room. Be ready to stop. Do not frighten them by sounding your horn or revving your engine. [Picture next page]

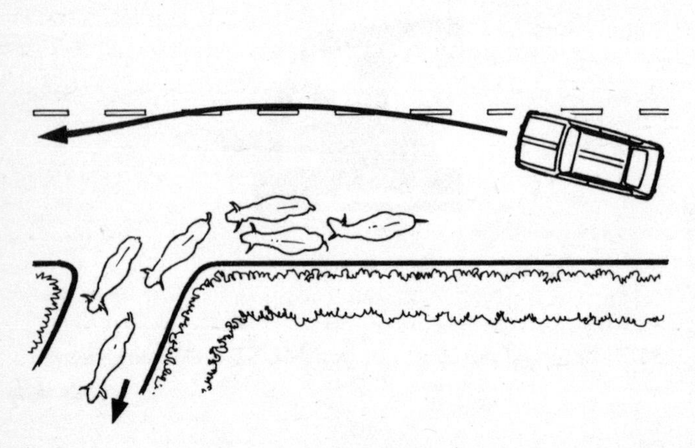

Give animals plenty of room.

(rule 80)

120 *Glasses:* if you need glasses or contact lenses to read the number plate of a vehicle 20.5 metres (67 feet) away 'you MUST wear them when driving'.

(rule 34)

121 *Signs:*

(a) overhead electric cable;
(b) roundabout;
(c) uneven road.

122 *Signs:*

(a) vehicles may pass either side to reach same destination;
(b) mini-roundabout.

123 *Signals:* the red stop light signals at the rear of the car.

***124** *Motorway lanes:* the inner lane is for driving; the middle lane is for overtaking slower vehicles on the inner lane, and the outer lane is for overtaking slower vehicles on the middle lane. Always 'return to the lane to your left when you have passed them'.

hard shoulder

driving lane

middle lane for overtaking slower vehicles on the left

outer lane for overtaking vehicles in middle lane

(rule 164)

***125** *Lines:* you may cross only:

(a) when you need to get in and out of property or a side road;

(b) when you have to avoid something stationary blocking your lane.

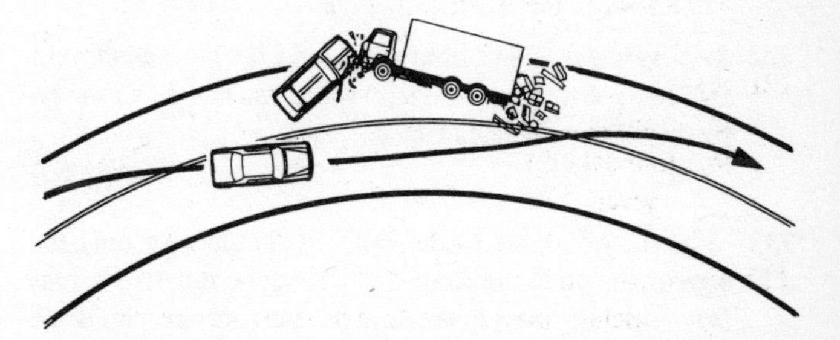

(rule 84)

126 *Overtaking:* when you are being overtaken, do not increase your speed. In fact, you may need to slow down to allow the overtaking vehicle past.

(rule 104)

***127** *Junctions:* you MUST stop at the line. Wait for a safe gap in the traffic before moving off.

(rule 109)

128 *Direction signs:* it is a *diversion route* sign.

***129** *Zebra crossings:* once a pedestrian has actually stepped on to a zebra crossing he or she has right of way; until then the traffic does not have to stop.

(rules 11 & 71)

130 *Road markings:* a broken yellow line means *limited waiting*. The time you can wait and the hours for which the limits are in force are shown on nearby blue plates.

131 *Motorway parking:* you must *never* park:
(a) on the *carriageway* itself;
(b) on the *slip roads;*
(c) or on the *central reservation;*
but you may park on the hard shoulder in an emergency.

(rules 180, 183)

132 *Slow vehicles:* don't hold up a long queue behind you. Pull in or slow down and stop when you can do so safely, so that faster vehicles can go past.

(rule 53)

***133** *Signals:* no – the Code says you should give only the signals shown in the Code and waving pedestrians across isn't one of them! Waving people across could be dangerous if another vehicle is approaching.

(rule 71)

134 *Roundabouts:*

(*a*) approach the roundabout in the right-hand lane and indicate right on approach;

(*b*) keep to the right-hand lane in the roundabout;

(*c*) keep the right-hand signal going until you have passed the exit *before* the one to be taken; then change to the left-hand indicator for leaving the roundabout.

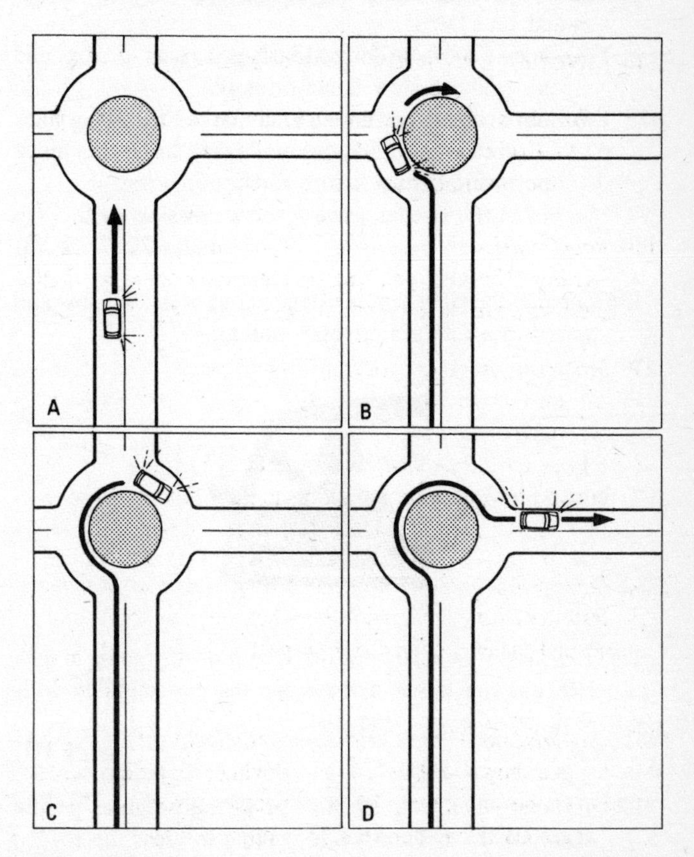

(rule 124)

135 *Estate cars:* the Code says that you should *not* do this.
(rule 42)

***136** *Signs:*
(a) level crossing *with* barrier or gate;
(b) level crossing *without* barrier or gate.

137 *Zebra crossings:* drivers approaching zebra crossings should:
(a) keep a look-out for pedestrians waiting to cross and be ready to slow down or stop;
(b) not overtake within the area marked by zigzag lines – even where there are no zigzag lines, they must not overtake just before a zebra crossing;
(c) in traffic queues leave a zebra crossing clear.
(rules 71, 72 & 73)

138 *Signals:* the right arm is extended out of the window and waved in a forward circular motion.

139 *Junctions:* obviously this driver is probably going to turn left, but you should not assume that he definitely will. Wait and see, to make sure.
(rule 111)

***140** *Textured paving:* 'to let blind or partially-sighted people know where to stand while waiting to cross the road'.
(rule 20)

141 *Stopping distances:* overall stopping distances increase greatly with:

(a) wet and slippery roads;
(b) poor brakes;
(c) poor tyres; and
(d) tired drivers.

(rule 57)

***142** *Motorway prohibitions:* the following are not allowed on motorways:

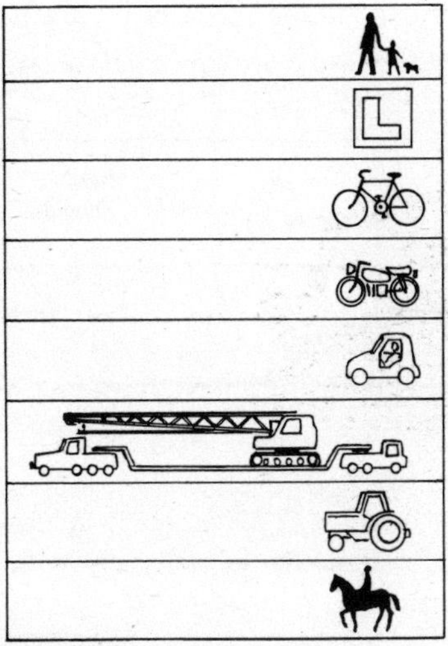

(a) pedestrians;
(b) learner drivers;
(c) cyclists;
(d) riders of motor-cycles under 50cc;
(e) some invalid carriages;
(f) slow-moving vehicles;
(g) agricultural vehicles;
(h) horse riders

(rule 155)

143 *Signs:* no waiting at any time (except for loading or unloading).

144 *Seat belts:* the Code specifies 'a baby carrier, child seat, harness or booster seat appropriate to the child's weight.'

(rule 41)

***145** *Motorway procedure:*

(*a*) watch for a *safe gap* in the traffic;

(*b*) *increase your speed* to match that of the traffic on the inside lane of the motorway, but give way to traffic already on it;

(*c*) then *merge out* into the inside lane;

(*d*) after joining the motorway, stay in the left-hand lane long enough to *get used* to the speed of the traffic before trying to overtake.

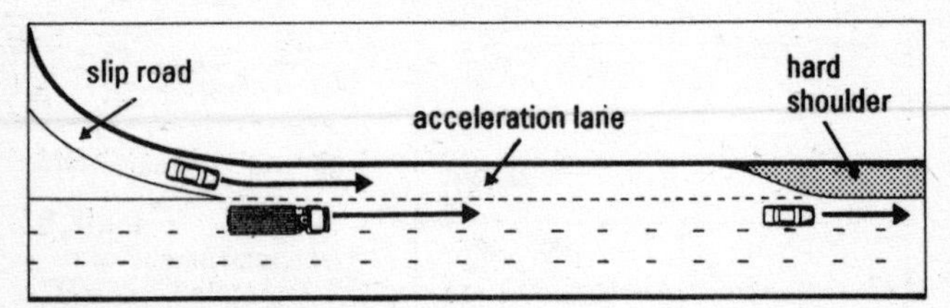

1. Drive into acceleration lane

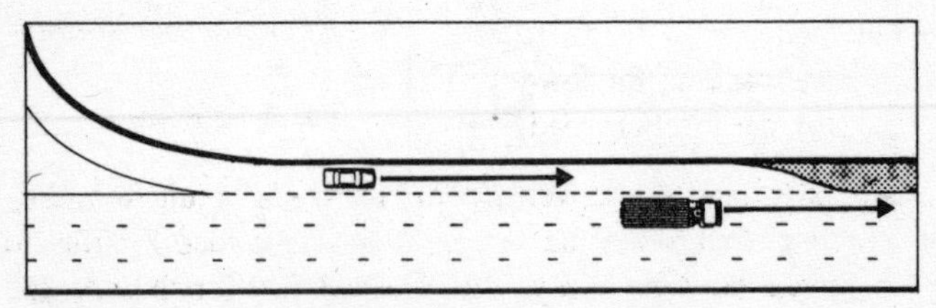

2. Watch for a safe gap, then accelerate

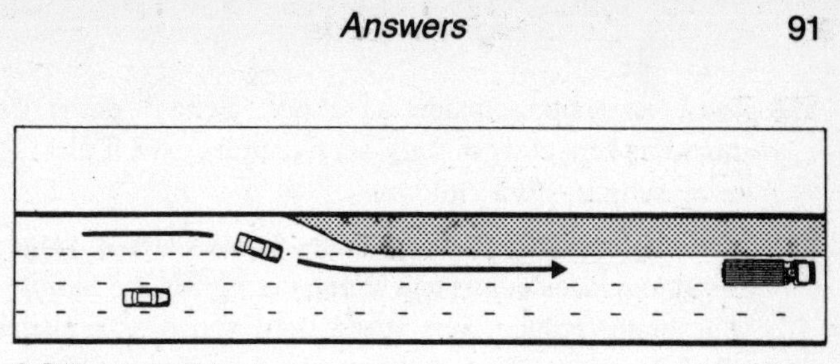

3. Pull out smoothly

(rules 158, 159 & 160)

146 *Single track roads:* a single track road is one which is only wide enough for one *line of vehicles*, usually provided with places for passing and overtaking. Drivers going downhill should give way to vehicles coming *uphill.*

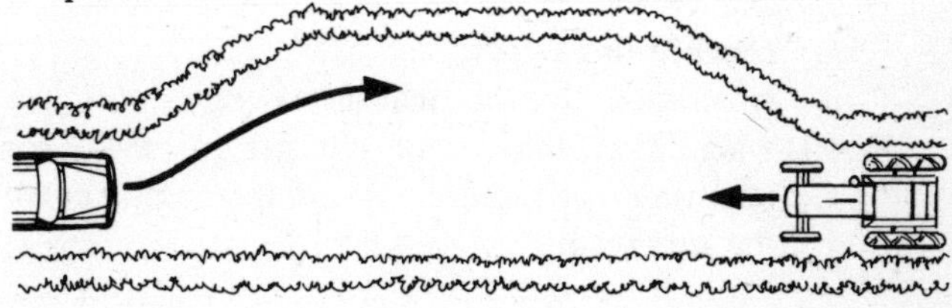

(rule 82)

147 *Bus and tram lanes:* outside the indicated period of operation, all vehicles may use a bus or tram lane.

(rule 97)

148 *Signs:*

(a) parking for towed caravans;
(b) no through road.

149 *Junctions:* if long vehicles are turning at a junction, they may need to use the whole width of the road in order to make the turn and you must watch out for this.

(rule 107)

150 *Road markings:* outside a school. School entrances should be kept clear of stationary vehicles even if picking up or setting down children.

151 *Motorway signals:* flashing amber lights warn of danger ahead, e.g. accident or fog. When the signals are flashing you should reduce your speed until you pass a signal which is not flashing and you are sure it is safe to go faster.

(rule 171)

152 *Overtaking:* on motorways, you must beware of vehicles coming up from behind much more quickly than you think, and ensure that the lane you will be using is clear for a long way ahead and behind.

(rule 168)

***153** *Turning right:*

(a) check your *mirrors;*
(b) when safe, give the right-turn *signal;*
(c) when safe, move into the gap in the *central reservation* and *wait* there until it is safe to cross to the side road.

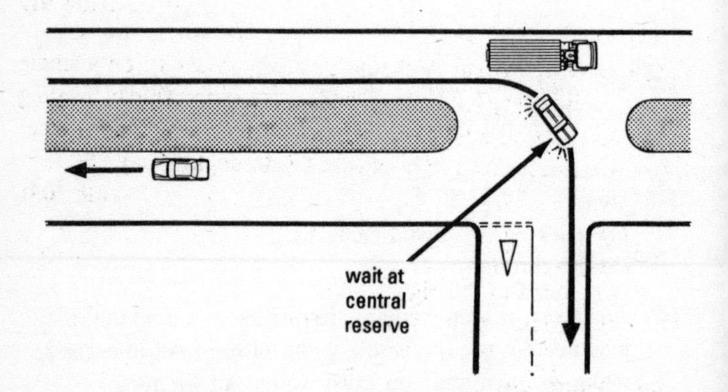

(rules 117 & 120)

***154** *Hats for horse riders:* you should wear an approved safety helmet and fasten it securely – and children under 14 MUST wear hard hats.

(rule 218)

***155** *Signs:*
(a) no right turn;
(b) no left turn;
(c) no U-turns.

156 *Signals:* the driver intends to *pull in to the left, turn left, or stop on the left.*

157 *Motorway overtaking:* the car in the distance. The outside lane is for *overtaking only;* having overtaken, he ought to have returned to the middle, and then to the inside lane, as soon as possible.

(rule 169)

158 *Lanes:* rule 91 which states 'In a traffic hold-up, do not try to "jump the queue" by cutting into another lane or by overtaking the vehicles in front of you'.

(rule 91)

159 *Overtaking:* car A should give way to car B: on a single carriageway road you should give way to vehicles coming towards you before you pass parked vehicles or other obstructions on the left-hand side of the road.

(rule 105)

160 *Signs:*
(a) bend to the right;
(b) double bend, first to left.

161 *Pedestrians:*
(a) in crowded shopping streets;

(b) near bus and tram stops;
(c) near a parked milk-float or mobile shop;
(d) near stationary vehicles.

(rule 63)

162 *Road markings:* it means stop here; it might be found, for example, at a traffic light. **(rules 109, 114)**

163 *Buses:* whenever you can do so in safety you should give way to buses, especially when they are signalling to pull away from bus stops – and keep an eye open for people getting off and crossing the road. **(rule 79)**

***164** *Level crossings:* in its general advice about level crossings, the Code says that you must never:
(a) drive 'nose-to-tail' over it;
(b) drive on to a crossing unless it is *clear on the other side;*
(c) stop *on* or *immediately beyond* any crossing.
(rule 225)

***165** *Police stopping procedures:* they will try to attract your attention by flashing their headlights or blue light, or by sounding their siren or horn. Then 'a police officer will direct you to pull over to the side by pointing and using the left indicator'. You MUST respond by stopping as soon as it is safe to do so, and you must switch off your engine. **(rule 78)**

166 *Horn:* when your vehicle is stationary on the road, you may only use your horn when a moving vehicle poses a danger. **(rule 136)**

167 *Mini-roundabouts:*
(a) the sign is a blue circle with three arrows going round it in white;
(b) no: the same rules 123-127 must be obeyed. **(rule 128)**

168 *Signs:*
(a) two-way traffic straight ahead;
(b) two-way traffic crosses one-way road;
(c) give priority to oncoming traffic.

169 *Speed limits: 60 m.p.h.* – providing of course no signs show otherwise. **(rule 54 and table)**

170 *Kerb markings:* double yellow flashes on the kerb mean *no loading* or *unloading* during every working day, with details of times shown on the plates.

171 *Motorway signals:* it warns that the outside lane is closed ahead. **(rule 171)**

172 *Breakdowns:* the triangle should be placed on the road at least 50 metres before the obstruction and on the same side of the road. Also use your hazard warning lights. **(rule 150)**

***173** *Learner motorcyclists:* no; you must display L-plates, but you must also first take basic training with an approved training body, unless you are exempt. **(rule 37)**

***174** *Flashing amber lights:* drive carefully – they 'warn of a slow-moving vehicle (such as a road gritter or tractor) or a vehicle which has broken down'. **(rule 77)**

175 *Signs:* services available at Puddleworth are:
(a) petrol;
(b) cafeteria;
(c) facilities for disabled.

***176** *Sleepiness:* by driving with plenty of fresh air in your vehicle. If you become tired on a journey, stop and rest at a suitable parking place. Walk around. On a motorway, stop at a service area, or leave the motorway. **(rules 32 & 162)**

177 *Motorway procedure:* you should 'stay in the left-hand lane long enough to get used to the *speed of traffic* before overtaking'. **(rule 160)**

178 *Single track roads:*
(a) make use of the passing places to allow other traffic to pass or overtake;
(b) give way to vehicles coming uphill whenever possible;
(c) do not park in passing places. **(rule 82)**

***179** *Seat belts:* the Code sets out the legal requirement that for a child over 3 years old an adult seat belt must, if available, be worn. 'An appropriate child restraint is a baby carrier, child seat, harness or booster seat appropriate to the child's weight'. **(rules 40, 41)**

180 *Box junctions:* have criss-cross yellow lines painted on the road.

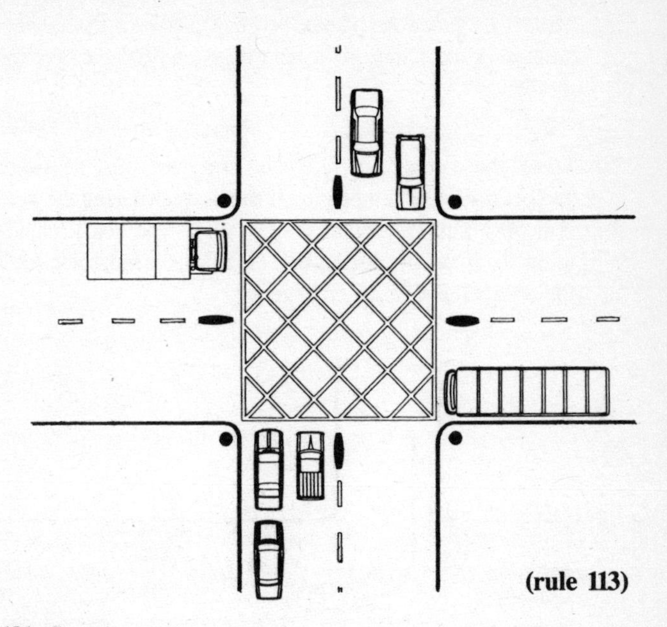

(rule 113)

181 *Signs:*

(a) no vehicle with over 12 seats (except school and work buses);
(b) no vehicle over 32 feet;
(c) no goods vehicles over 7.5 tonnes;
(d) low flying aircraft or sudden aircraft noise.

182 *Signals:* right arm fully extended, out of the window, palm forwards.

***183** *Motorway junctions:* 'make sure you are in the correct lane; at some junctions a lane may lead directly off the motorway'.

(rule 165)

184 *Lines:* these areas separate you from oncoming traffic or protect traffic turning right. If the line bordering the area is broken you may enter it only when you see it is safe to do so. If the bordering line is solid you must not enter the area except in an emergency.

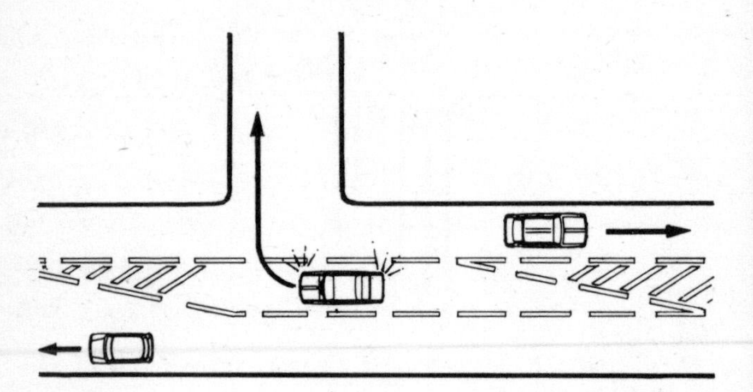

(rule 86)

***185** *Pedestrian crossings:* zigzag lines show where you must *not overtake* or park at or near the crossing.

(rules 72 & 138)

***186** *Junctions:* you should normally keep the other vehicle to your *right*, and pass *behind* it (offside to offside), not forgetting to *check* for other traffic before completing the turn. **(rule 118)**

187 *Signs:* offside half of a car coming towards you, throwing up stones with its tyres, on a white background, surrounded by a red triangle.

***188** *Pelican crossings:* it means you must give way to any pedestrians on the crossing; otherwise you may proceed. **(rule 74)**

189 *Traffic lights:* red and amber mean stop.

190 *Signs:*
(*a*) with-flow bus and cycle lane;
(*b*) contra-flow bus lane.

***191** *Horse riders:* there are three points:
- Look out for their signals;
- Remember that a horse rider might not move to the centre of the road before turning right;
- Take extra care when the riders are children.

(rules 80 & 81)

***192** *Traffic light failure:* you may proceed but do so with caution. **(rule 116)**

193 *Direction signs:* the black border signifies that the directions shown are to *local places* on a non-primary route.

194 *Signs:*
(*a*) no vehicles;
(*b*) no stopping (clearway).

195 *Motorway lanes:* except in prescribed circumstances, goods vehicles with an operating weight of more than 7.5 tonnes, or any vehicle drawing a trailer or a bus or coach longer than 12 metres may not use the outside lane of a three-lane motorway.

(rule 166)

196 *Lanes:* they are the short broken white lines which divide the road into lanes. Keep between them.

(rule 87)

197 *Overtaking:*

(*a*) if you would have to cross or straddle double white lines with a solid line nearer to you;

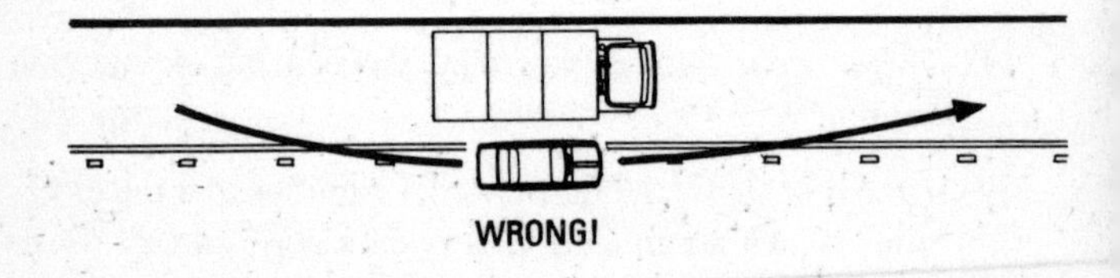

(*b*) if you are within the zigzag area at a pedestrian crossing;

(*c*) after a 'no overtaking' sign and until the end of the restriction. **(rule 106)**

198 *Dangerous goods:* you should:

1 Follow the general advice for accidents (rule 153) and:

2 Switch off engines and don't smoke;

3 Keep uninjured people well away from the vehicle and any dangerous substances;

4 Give the emergency services all the information you can about the vehicle's labels and other markings.

(rule 154)

199 *Signs:*
(*a*) no vehicles over 7′6″ wide;
(*b*) axle weight limit 2 tonnes;
(*c*) no vehicles over 14′6″ high.

***200** *Speed limits:* the presence of street lights indicates that the speed limit is *30 m.p.h.* unless any signs show other limits.

(rule 54)

***201** *Junctions:* stop. It is found at stop signs.

(rule 109)

202 *Motorway cruising:* you should 'make sure that your vehicle is fit to cruise at speed, has correct tyre pressures and enough fuel, oil and water to get you at least to the next service area. See that the windscreen, windows, mirrors, lights and reflectors are clean and that the windscreen washer bottle is topped up. You MUST make sure that any load you are carrying or towing is secure.'

(rule 157)

203 *Lights:* you should, to quote the Code, 'use your headlights or front fog lights when visibility is seriously reduced'. (By 'seriously' the Code means visibility reduced to less than 100 metres.)

(rule 131)

***204** *Motorway procedure:* you would normally reach a destination on the right by leaving the motorway via a slip road on your left.

(rule 185)

205 *Signs:*
(*a*)a hump bridge:
(*b*)an opening or swing bridge.

206 *Herding animals:* keep the herd to the left of the road; the Code adds: 'If possible, send another person along the road to warn other road users, for example at bends and the brows of hills'. **(rule 214)**

***207** *Road markings:*

(a) a lane line has *short markings with long gaps;*

(b) a hazard warning line has *long markings with short gaps;*

(c) a centre line has *markings and gaps of about equal length.*

(white lines on the road)

208 *Motorway stopping:* other than in a traffic queue the only circumstances under which you may stop on a motorway are:

(a) in an *emergency;*

(b) when you are *signalled* to do so by the police, an emergency sign or flashing red lights. **(rule 179)**

209 *Signs:* the sign shows a *boy and girl* in a *red triangle* with *'patrol'* underneath, and some have *amber flashing* lights.

***210** *Stopping distances:* the minimum overall stopping distance for a good car with an alert driver on dry roads travelling at 60 m.p.h. is *73 metres* (240 feet).

(rule 57)

211 *Reversing: 'Never* reverse from a side road into a main road.'

(rule 130)

212 *Direction signs:* the sign shows the direction to the M10 which joins the M1.

***213** *Overtaking:* you MUST NOT overtake.

(rule 106)

214 *Signals:* he uses his *right flashing indicators.*

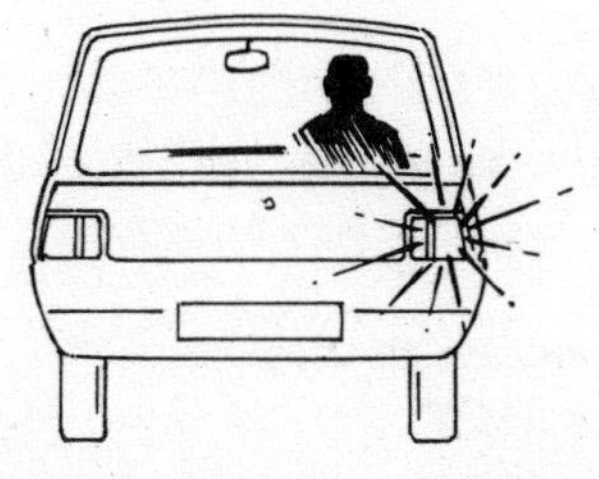

215 *Motorway slip roads:* stay in that lane until it becomes part of the motorway.

(rule 159)

216 *Signs:*

(a) traffic lights ahead;
(b) failure of light signals.

217 *Documents:* in this case you may present these documents, at any police station you select, within 7 days. **(the Road User and the Law)**

218 *Signs:*
(*a*) no entry for vehicular traffic;
(*b*) location of level crossing without barrier.

219 *Motorway procedure:* no, traffic on slip roads should always give way to traffic already on the motorway. **(rule 158)**

220 *Broken lines:* this line is a hazard warning line, but you may cross it if you can see that the road well ahead is clear. In a place such as illustrated, you would probably need to wait till you could see more. **(rule 83)**

221 *Overtaking:* you must 'take extra care at night and in poor visibility when it is harder to judge speed and distance'. **(rule 99)**

222 *Turning right:* car A, i.e. just left of the middle of the road. **(rule 117)**

***223** *Accidents:* in such an accident:
1 you must **STOP**:
2 you must *either:*
(*a*) give *your own and the vehicle owner's name and address* and the *car registration number,* and show the *insurance certificate*, to anyone reasonably wanting them, including the police; *or*
(*b*) *report* the accident to the *police* within 24 hours, and produce *the insurance certificate* for them within seven days.

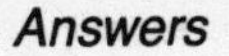

(the Road User and the Law)

224 *Signs:*
- *(a)* no motor vehicles;
- *(b)* no overtaking;
- *(c)* slippery road;
- *(d)* quayside or riverbank.

225 *Signs:*
- *(a)* give priority to vehicles from opposite direction;
- *(b)* [you have] priority over vehicles from opposite direction.

Notice that on both signs it is the arrow in *red* that shows from which direction traffic must cede priority.

226 *Signals:* left hand fully extended to the left, palm forwards.

***227** *Tramways:* there are seven main points:

- Do not enter a road or lane reserved for trams;
- Take extra care where tram tracks cross from one side of the road to the other;
- At tram stops with platforms you MUST follow the route shown by the road signs and markings;
- Don't drive between a tram and the left-hand kerb at a tram stop without a platform;
- Take extra care on a bicycle or motorcycle when riding near tram tracks, especially if the road is wet;
- Don't park where your vehicle would be in the way of trams or would force other drivers to get in the way;
- Always give way to trams.

(rules 235, 236, 237, 238, 239, 240)

228 *Lanes:*

(a) check your *mirrors;*

(b) if safe, *signal;*

(c) move over, making sure you will not force *another vehicle* to swerve or slow down. **(rules 89 & 168)**

***229** *General:* pedestrians: where there is no footpath the Code advises pedestrians to walk on the side *facing* oncoming traffic so that they can see vehicles approaching. **(rules 2 & 70)**

***230** *Box junctions:* you MUST NOT enter a box junction if your exit road or lane from it is not clear, but you may enter the box when you want to turn right, and are prevented from doing so only by oncoming traffic or by vehicles waiting to make a right turn. **(rule 113)**

***231** *Stopping distances:* the overall stopping distance with a good car, dry road and alert driver at 70 m.p.h. is *96 metres* (315 feet) roughly equivalent to *twenty-four* car lengths. **(rule 57)**

***232** *Learner drivers:* there are three criteria. The accompanying driver:

- Must be at least 21 years old;
- Must have held a full British licence for the type of car (manual or automatic) for at least three years; and
- Must still hold that licence. **(rule 36)**

***233** *Traffic lights:* the red light means stop but traffic wishing to filter *left* may do so if the way is clear.

234 *Opening doors:* you must check that no one is *close enough to be hit* by the door, especially pedestrians, cyclists and motorcyclists. **(rule 137)**

235 *Breakdowns:* you should try to get your vehicle off the road if possible. **(rule 149)**

236 *Signs:* the no entry sign is a red disc with a white horizontal bar across the middle.

237 *Signs:*
(a) cattle;
(b) wild animals;
(c) wild horses or ponies;
(d) accompanied horses or ponies.

238 *Pedestrians:* the pedestrian. **(rule 68)**

239 *Road markings:* a single yellow line means *no waiting*. The actual period of time covered will be shown on nearby *plates*, and is roughly *every working day*.

240 *Roundabouts:* long vehicles, cyclists and horse riders. Cyclists and horse riders will often keep to the left, even if they are indicating right to show that they are continuing round the roundabout. **(rules 126, 127)**

241 *Level crossings:* the Code says that first you should get *everyone out* of the car and clear of the crossing, and then *telephone* the signalman. After that, if time permits, you should try to get the car *off the crossing;* however, if the alarm sounds or the amber light comes on, or you hear a train, get clear of the crossing. **(rule 230)**

***242** *Junctions:*

(a) *approach with care;*
(b) check your road *position* and *speed;*
(c) watch out for *cyclists, motorcyclists* and *pedestrians* before you turn;
(d) watch out for *long vehicles*, which may be needing extra room for turning. **(rule 107)**

***243** *Accidents:* in an accident causing damage to another vehicle or roadside property, or harm to an animal:

(a) you must stop;
(b) you must give your *name, address* and *car registration number*, and the *name and address of the car's owner*, to anyone reasonably requiring them; or
(c) you must report the accident to the *police within 24 hours.* **(the Road User and the Law)**

***244** *Signs:* the level crossing with barrier or gate sign shows a gate printed black on a white background, and surrounded by a red triangle.

245 *Zebra crossings:* once the pedestrian has actually stepped on to the crossing, he or she has right of way. **(rule 71)**

246 *Motorway driving:*

(a) drive at a steady cruising speed within the capability of your vehicle and of yourself;
(b) do not forget the speed limits for the motorway or for your vehicle;
(c) keep a safe distance from the vehicle in front of you;

(*d*) on wet or icy roads, or in fog, leave a bigger gap between you and the vehicle in front. **(rule 161)**

***247** *Level crossings:* where a railway telephone is provided you should *phone the signal operator* for permission to cross. When the crossing is clear, phone again to report. **(rule 229)**

***248** *Lights:* you should dip your headlamps:
(*a*) when meeting other vehicles or road users;
(*b*) if you are close behind another vehicle;
(*c*) if you are in a built-up area.

(rule 132)

249 *Signs:*
(*a*) maximum speed limit 30 m.p.h.;
(*b*) national speed limit applies;
(*c*) minimum speed limit 30 m.p.h.;
(*d*) end of minimum speed limit.

***250** *Tyres:* the Law demands that your tyres are *suitable*, properly *inflated*, have a tread depth of *at least 1.6mm*, and are free from cuts and defects. **(the Road User and the Law)**

251 *Road markings:* it marks an area of road you MUST NOT enter except in an emergency. **(rule 86)**

252 *Dangerous goods:* it tells you that there is a dangerous substance being carried and that it is *poisonous.*

253 *Level crossings:* the procedure for such a crossing is:
1 Stop and check *no train* is coming.
2 Then *telephone* the signal operator.

3 Open *both* gates.
4 Check *again* that no train is coming.
5 Drive across quickly.
6 Close *both* gates.
7 Finally, *telephone* the signal operator again.

(rule 233)

254 *Hazard lights:* yes, but only on a motorway or unrestricted dual carriageway to warn drivers behind you of a hazard or obstruction ahead – and only for long enough to make sure they have been seen. **(rule 134)**

255 *Passengers:* you must not carry passengers in such numbers or in such a manner as is likely to cause danger of injury to yourself or others.

(the Road User and the Law)

WRONG!

256 *Signs:* the *unspecified hazard sign* shows an exclamation mark printed in black on a white background and surrounded by a red triangle. Sometimes a plate below will state the nature of the hazard.

257 *Moving off:*

(a) check your mirrors;
(b) signal, if necessary;
(c) look round;
(d) move off only when it is safe to do so.

(rule 48)

***258** *Traffic lights:* you should *stop;* 'you may go on only if the amber appears after you have *crossed the stop line* or are so close to it that to pull up might cause an accident'.

(rule 114)

***259** *Roadworks:* the Code's advice concerning roadworks is:

- Take special care;
- Watch out for all signs and act on them;
- Use your mirrors and get into the correct lane in good time;
- Do not switch lanes to overtake queuing traffic;
- Do not drive through an area marked off by traffic cones;
- Watch out for traffic entering or leaving the area where work is going on – but don't let yourself be distracted by what is going on there.
- 'You MUST NOT exceed any temporary maximum speed limit'.

(rules 147, 148)

260 *Signs and signals:* the flashing red lights may be at level crossings, lifting bridges, air fields, fire stations, etc., and on motorways. These alternately flashing red lights mean *you must stop.*

***261** *Cyclists:* the Code advises that a cyclist should:

- 'wear a cycle helmet which conforms to recognised safety standards'
- avoid flowing garments that could become entangled in the wheels;
- in daylight and poor visibility wear light coloured or *fluorescent* clothing so that you can be seen;
- at night wear *reflective* materials.

(rules 190, 191)

262 *Signs:*
- *(a)* turn left ahead;
- *(b)* turn left;
- *(c)* ahead only;
- *(d)* keep left;
- *(e)* one way traffic (note the difference between this and *(c)*);
- *(f)* one way street.

263 *Road markings: give way* to traffic on major road.
(rule 110)

264 *Motorway sleepiness:* make sure there is plenty of fresh air in the vehicle, or stop at a service area or turn off at an exit and find a safe place to stop.
(rule 162)

265 *Signs:* an inverted triangle with a red surround and wide red and white sloping stripes across it.

266 *First aid:* if breathing has stopped:
1. Remove any *obstruction* in mouth.
2. Keep head *tilted backwards* and, if breathing does not start,
3. Pinch the *nostrils* together and *blow into the mouth* until chest rises,
4. Repeat every *four seconds* until the casualty can breathe unaided.

(First aid, at the back of the Highway Code)

267 *Driving prohibitions:* footway, footpath, bridle-way, or cycle track at any time, or a bus or cycle lane during its hours of operation.

(The Road User and the Law)

268 *Driving along:* you should normally drive on the *left;* exceptions are: when road markings indicate otherwise, when you intend to overtake, or turn right, or when you have to pass parked vehicles or pedestrians in the road.

(rule 49)

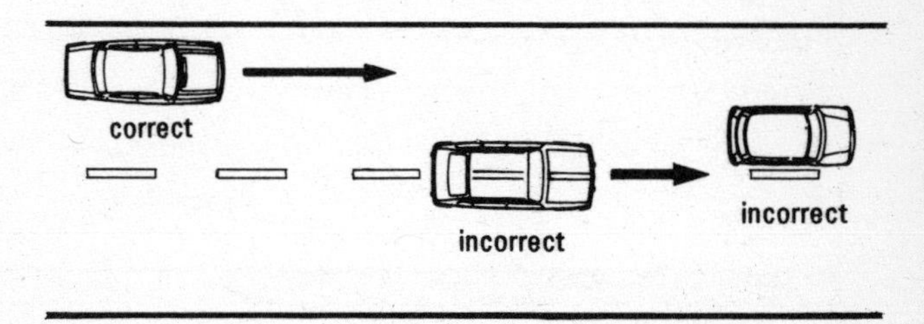

269 *Police signals:*

(a) stop (to vehicles from the *front*);
(b) come on (to vehicles from the front);
(c) stop (to vehicles from front and behind).

***270** *Motorway procedure:*

(a) If you are not already in the left-hand lane, check your mirrors, signal and move into it well before your turning – and, if necessary, reduce speed;
(b) check your mirrors again, signal left and move into the slip road lane, that is the short parallel part before the exit itself;
(c) keep signalling and slow well down as the slip road bears away from the motorway – remember that some slip roads have sharp bends.

[Picture next page]

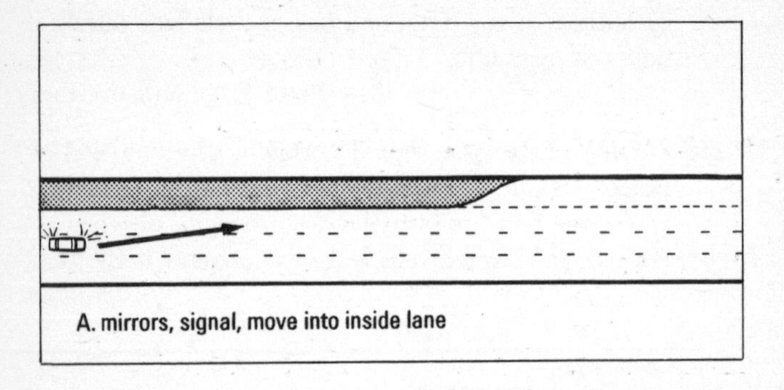

A. mirrors, signal, move into inside lane

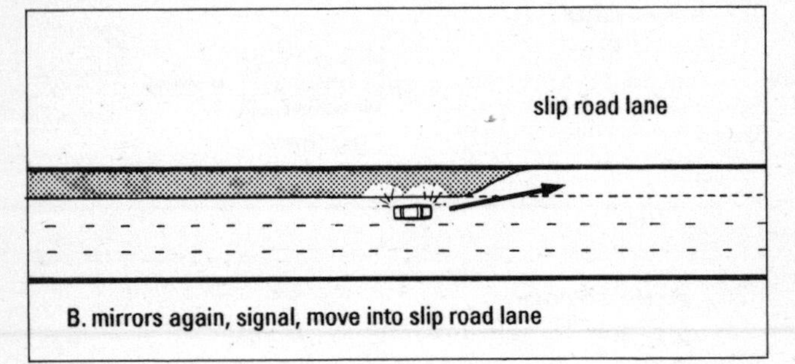

B. mirrors again, signal, move into slip road lane

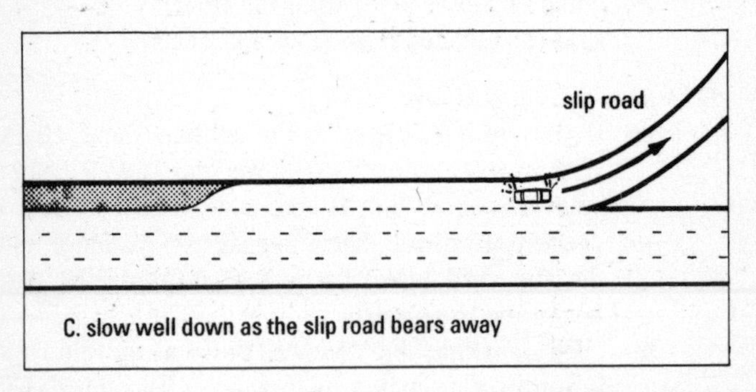

C. slow well down as the slip road bears away

(rules 185, 186)

271 *Insurance:* you must have, at least, third party insurance covering your use of the vehicle.

(the Road User and the Law)

272 *Signs:* 'no motor vehicles' sign shows a motorcycle printed above a car, in black on a white background, surrounded by a red circle.

273 *Schools:*

(a) drive slowly near a school;
(b) pay heed to flashing amber lights beneath 'school' signs;
(c) look out for children getting on or off buses;
(d) you *MUST* stop when signalled to do so by a school crossing patrol.

(rules 65, 66)

***274** *Road markings:* it means *no crossing* of the solid line if it is nearer to the driver than the broken line.

***275** *Roadworks speed limits:* 'you must NOT exceed any temporary maximum speed limit'.

(rule 148)

***276** *Parking at night:* a car may be parked at night without lights provided that:

(a) it is parked on a road within a *30 m.p.h.* speed limit;
(b) it is at least *10 metres* from the nearest junction;
(c) it is facing the same way as the direction of the traffic flow on its own side of the road.

(rule 143)

***277** *Overtaking:* yes, provided you can do so safely

but remember you must not enter a bus or tram lane during its period of operation in order to do so, unless signs allow this. **(rules 97 & 102)**

278 *Lights:* the Code says you MUST:

- use sidelights between sunset and sunrise;
- use *headlights* between half an hour after sunset and half an hour before sunrise where the road is not adequately lit;
- use headlights or front fog lights when visibility is seriously reduced (this means when you cannot see for more than 100 metres). **(rule 131)**

279 *Roundabouts:* unless signs or road markings indicate differently, use the most appropriate lane on approach and through the roundabout. **(rule 124)**

280 *Road markings:* a double yellow line means *no waiting*. The actual period of time covered will be shown on nearby plates, and the restrictions apply roughly every working day and additional times.

281 *Pedestrians:* give them *plenty of room,* keep to a *low speed*, and be especially careful on a *left-hand bend.* **(rule 70)**

282 *Parking on road:*

(a) stop as close as possible to the side;
(b) make sure the handbrake is on firmly;
(c) switch off the engine;
(d) lock the car;
(e) at night, switch off your headlights. **(rule 137)**

***283** *Motorway breakdown:*

(a) the way to the nearest emergency telephone is shown by arrows on posts at the back of the hard shoulder;
(b) 'you MUST NOT try to cross the motorway'. **(rule 183)**

***284** *Fog:* in daytime fog you would use your *headlights (or front fog lights*). **(rule 131)**

285 *Reversing:* make absolutely sure there are no pedestrians (especially children) or obstructions in the road behind. Be particularly careful about the 'blind' area behind you which is the area which you cannot see from the driving seat. **(rule 129)**

***286** *Fog:* start by asking yourself if your journey is essential. Then allow extra time for it. Check that your lights, including the brake lights, are working, and that lights, windscreen and windows are clean.

- See and be seen. Use dipped headlights and windscreen wipers and demisters. In very thick fog use front or rear fog lights.
- Check your mirrors, slow down, and keep a safe distance.
- Do not hang on to someone else's tail lights.
- Watch your speed – you may be going faster than you think.
- When you slow down, use your brakes so that your brake lights warn drivers behind you.
- Pay attention to roadside fog warning signals even if the road is clear. Fog can be patchy, and there may be a thick bank of it ahead. **(rules 58, 133)**

287 *Signs:* the level crossing without gate or barrier sign shows an antique-type steam engine, printed in black on a white background, inside a red triangle.

288 *Motorcyclists:* the Code states that when on a motorcycle, scooter or moped, you must wear a safety helmet of *approved design* which must be *'fastened securely'.* This rule applies to a pillion passenger as well as to the rider. **(rule 30)**

***289** *Accidents:* if you are first on the scene of an accident, you should:

- *warn* other traffic, for example by turning on your hazard warning lights;
- *ask* other drivers to turn off their engines and put out any cigarettes;
- *call* police and emergency services at once;
- *leave* injured people in their vehicles *unless they are in immediate danger* from fire or explosion;
- *do not* remove a motorcyclist's helmet unless it is essential;
- *be prepared* to give first aid as found in the back of the Code;
- *move* uninjured people away from the accident to a place of safety;
- *stay* at the scene until the emergency services arrive.

(rule 153)

290 *Motorway procedure:* your speed may be higher than you think, e.g. 50 m.p.h. may feel like 30 m.p.h., so check your speed on your speedometer. **(rule 186)**

291 *Breakdowns:* it should be placed at least 150 metres before the obstruction, on the hard shoulder. On no account try to place it on part of the main carriageway. Also use your hazard warning lights. **(rules 150, 183)**

292 *Motorcyclists:*
(a) you may only carry *one* passenger; who
(b) must sit on a securely fastened, *proper seat;*
(c) must have proper *foot rests;*
(d) must wear an approved *safety helmet.*

(the Road User and the Law)

***293** *Parking:* a 'clearway' is a road on which there is no stopping; on an urban clearway stopping is banned between the times shown on the notices, except to set down or pick up passengers.

(rule 138)

294 *Documents:* before driving, you must make sure that:

1 The *tax disc* is displayed.
2 Your car is properly *insured.*
3 You have a current *driving licence.*
4 You have a current *MOT test certificate.*

(the Road User and the Law)

295 *Driving along:*

(a) when driving along you should normally be on the *left*, but; when

b) turning right, you should be *just left of the middle* of the road, (or in the space marked for right-turning traffic). 'If possible leave room for other vehicles to pass on the left'. **(rules 49, 117)**

***296** *Cyclists:* The Code says: 'You MUST NOT cycle on the pavement'. **(rule 192)**

***297** *Crawler lanes:* on some hills, particularly very long or steep ones. You should use this lane if you are driving a slow moving vehicle, or to let faster vehicles behind you overtake. **(rule 88)**

298 *Seat belts:* the exempt people include:

(a) holders of medical exemption certificates;

(b) people making local deliveries from a vehicle adapted for that purpose.

(the Road User and the Law)

299 *Dual carriageways:* the right hand lane should be used only for overtaking or preparing to turn right.

(rule 94)

300 *Motorcyclists:* always keep a special look out for them. Remember they are more difficult to see than larger vehicles, but they have the same rights and are more vulnerable. Give them plenty of room, especially if you are driving a long vehicle or towing.

(rule 52)

Driving Instructors

It is wise to go to a Department of Transport approved driving instructor for lessons as you can be sure he is qualified and knows his job. Each such instructor has a *certificate of approval,* obtained only after passing a written and practical examination, which he will gladly show you on request.

Approved instructors are regularly checked by Department of Transport inspectors; you can get the names and addresses of local approved instructors by contacting a Department of Transport Office, or the A.A. or R.A.C.

Index

The references are to *question* numbers, not page numbers. Star questions are highlighted in bold.

The references are to *question* numbers, not page numbers. Star questions are highlighted in bold.

The references are to *question* numbers, not page numbers. Star questions are highlighted in bold.

MORE PAPERFRONT MOTORING TITLES

In the same series

CAR DRIVING IN 2 WEEKS

An ideal book for every learner driver who wants to get through the test first time; it has already helped millions.

The original author was formerly a Branch Manager with the British School of Motoring Ltd and later founded the **Right Way Schools of Motoring**. The book has since been completely revised and re-written and is further updated at every reprint to keep pace with the ever changing conditions of our roads.

What the critics say:

Daily Telegraph – "Immensely practical"
Motor – "A book worth having"
Autocar – "No learner could fail to benefit"
Highland News – "A bible for "L" drivers"

Uniform with this book

In the same series

What to Watch Out For When BUYING A USED CAR

Thousands of people buy second-hand cars each year. Sadly, many of them end up with vehicles which cost hundreds of pounds in repair bills. Make sure you're not one of them. Find out how to judge a car's merits, detect its faults and value it accurately. Whether you're buying from a private individual, from a car dealer or at auction, this book will save you money!

PASS YOUR MOTORCYCLE L-TEST

An immensely popular book, now in its third huge printing, from a life-long riding enthusiast. In a logical sequence it sets out everything you need to know to pass the Compulsory Basic Training Test and the Accompanied (or 'pursuit') Test but then takes you on to advanced riding techniques with much sound advice learned from years of experience in the saddle.

Uniform with this book

In the same series

LEARNING TO DRIVE IN PICTURES

The safe way to learn to drive: achieve car control *before* going on the road; get to grips with the *rules of the road*, tackled here in a progressive, logical order; gain essential knowledge on skidding, night driving and motorways; get into the way of *advanced safety thinking*, the planned avoidance of danger, that saves lives.

VERY ADVANCED DRIVING

Contains a wealth of indispensable advice on fast driving, overtaking, driving in bad weather, skidding and other emergencies.

What the critics say:

The Times – "...well-written, well-illustrated and very comprehensive"
Daily Telegraph – "...brisk, straightforward...outstanding value..."

Uniform with this book

In the same series

PASS YOUR MOT FIRST TIME

Around half the cars and light vans put in for the MOT Test in Great Britain *fail!* With this book anyone, mechanic or novice, can prevent failure, thus saving time, money and hassle. It enables you to run a mock test and establish exactly what may need attention *before* you submit your vehicle to the Testing Station. Step-by-step procedures are given for easy D-I-Y repairs, and garage attention is recommended where necessary. It has been written by a professional MOT tester who is in a unique position to know what are the most common causes of failure and the best ways to put them right.

TEACH YOUR SON OR DAUGHTER TO DRIVE

Learn to teach and be taught with this concise and well-illustrated book. Centred upon an in-depth analysis of the Highway Code, it provides an excellent companion to *Highway Code Questions and Answers*.

The emphasis is on safe handling and confidence which combine to ensure that all test requirements are mastered.

Uniform with this book

OUR PUBLISHING POLICY

HOW WE CHOOSE

Our policy is to consider every deserving manuscript and we can give special editorial help where an author is an authority on his subject but an inexperienced writer. We are rigorously selective in the choice of books we publish. We set the highest standards of editorial quality and accuracy. This means that a *Paperfront* is easy to understand and delightful to read. Where illustrations are necessary to convey points of detail, these are drawn up by a subject specialist artist from our panel.

HOW WE KEEP PRICES LOW

We aim for the big seller. This enables us to order enormous print runs and achieve the lowest price for you. Unfortunately, this means that you will not find in the *Paperfront* list any titles on obscure subjects of minority interest only. These could not be printed in large enough quantities to be sold for the low price at which we offer this series.

We sell almost all our *Paperfronts* at the same unit price. This saves a lot of fiddling about in our clerical departments and helps us to give you world-beating value. Under this system, the longer titles are offered at a price which we believe to be unmatched by any publisher in the world.

OUR DISTRIBUTION SYSTEM

Because of the competitive price, and the rapid turnover, *Paperfronts* are possibly the most profitable line a bookseller can handle. They are stocked by the best bookshops all over the world. It may be that your bookseller has run out of stock of a particular title. If so, he can order more from us at any time—we have a fine reputation for "same day" despatch, and we supply any order, however small (even a single copy), to any bookseller who has an account with us. We prefer you to buy from your bookseller, as this reminds him of the strong underlying public demand for *Paperfronts*. Members of the public who live in remote places, or who are housebound, or whose local bookseller is unco-operative, can order direct from us by post.

FREE

If you would like an up-to-date list of all *Paperfront* titles currently available, send a stamped self-addressed envelope to
ELLIOT RIGHT WAY BOOKS, BRIGHTON RD.,
LOWER KINGSWOOD, TADWORTH, SURREY, KT20 6TD, UK.